W9-CKT-770

Julia
Roberts

Titles in the People in the News series include:

PEOPLE
IN THE NEWS

Julia
Roberts

by Terri Dougherty

LUCENT BOOKS
SAN DIEGO, CALIFORNIA

THOMSON
GALE

Detroit • New York • San Diego • San Francisco
Boston • New Haven, Conn. • Waterville, Maine
London • Munich

Library of Congress Cataloging-in-Publication Data

Dougherty, Terri.
  Julia Roberts / by Terri Dougherty.
    p. cm. – (People in the news)
Includes bibliographical references and index.
Summary: Profiles the popular, Academy Award–winning actress who has been called "the most powerful celebrity on the planet" and "America's best movie star."
  ISBN 1-59018-139-5 (alk. paper)
1. Roberts, Julia, 1967–Juvenile literature. 2. Motion picture actors and actresses–United States–Biography–Juvenile literature. [1. Roberts, Julia, 1967– 2. Actors and actresses. 3. Women–Biography.] I. Title. II. People in the news (San Diego, Calif.)
  PN2287 .R63 D68 2003
  791.43'028'092—dc21

2001007418

Copyright © 2003 by Lucent Books,
an imprint of The Gale Group
10911 Technology Place, San Diego, CA 92127
Printed in the U.S.A.

Table of Contents

Foreword

FAME AND CELEBRITY are alluring. People are drawn to those who walk in fame's spotlight, whether they are known for great accomplishments or for notorious deeds. The lives of the famous pique public interest and attract attention, perhaps because their experiences seem in some ways so different from, yet in other ways so similar to, our own.

Newspapers, magazines, and television regularly capitalize on this fascination with celebrity by running profiles of famous people. For example, television programs such as *Entertainment Tonight* devote all of their programming to stories about entertainment and entertainers. Magazines such as *People* fill their pages with stories of the private lives of famous people. Even newspapers, newsmagazines, and television news frequently delve into the lives of well-known personalities. Despite the number of articles and programs, few provide more than a superficial glimpse at their subjects.

Lucent's People in the News series offers young readers a deeper look into the lives of today's newsmakers, the influences that have shaped them, and the impact they have had in their fields of endeavor and on other people's lives. The subjects of the series hail from many disciplines and walks of life. They include authors, musicians, athletes, political leaders, entertainers, entrepreneurs, and others who have made a mark on modern life and who, in many cases, will continue to do so for years to come.

These biographies are more than factual chronicles. Each book emphasizes the contributions, accomplishments, or deeds that have brought fame or notoriety to the individual and shows how that person has influenced modern life. Authors portray their subjects in a realistic, unsentimental light. For example, Bill Gates––the cofounder and chief executive officer of the software giant Microsoft—has been instrumental in making personal computers the most vital tool of the modern age. Few dispute his business savvy, his perseverance, or his technical expertise, yet critics say he is ruthless in his dealings with competitors and driven more by his desire to maintain Microsoft's dominance in the computer industry than by an interest in furthering technology.

In these books, young readers will encounter inspiring stories about real people who achieved success despite enormous obstacles. Oprah Winfrey—the most powerful, most watched, and wealthiest woman on television today—spent the first six years of her life in the care of her grandparents while her unwed mother sought work and a better life elsewhere. Her adolescence was colored by promiscuity, pregnancy at age fourteen, rape, and sexual abuse.

Each author documents and supports his or her work with an array of primary and secondary source quotations taken from diaries, letters, speeches, and interviews. All quotes are footnoted to show readers exactly how and where biographers derive their information and provide guidance for further research. The quotations enliven the text by giving readers eyewitness views of the life and accomplishments of each person covered in the People in the News series.

In addition, each book in the series includes photographs, annotated bibliographies, timelines, and comprehensive indexes. For both the casual reader and the student researcher, the People in the News series offers insight into the lives of today's newsmakers—people who shape the way we live, work, and play in the modern age.

Introduction

Julia

JULIA ROBERTS DIDN'T plan to become a superstar. She wasn't lured into acting by the pursuit of fame and money. She didn't consciously work at gaining the public's attention. She just wanted to be an actress, and a good one. Roberts found the profession interesting, exciting, challenging, and simply tried to do her best every time she set to work on a new role. The fame and money that came with her success surprised and challenged her.

Roberts's genuine personality and strong work ethic have worked in her favor. She's become one of the most popular celebrities in the world. Known for both her acting ability and intriguing personal life, Roberts's lifestyle has been shaped by the way she deals with her successes and failures as an actress, as well as the attention generated by her offscreen activities. Part Southern lady, part sassy free spirit, Roberts has become a successful Oscar-winning actress who thrives on the varied experiences her career offers.

Success came quickly to Roberts, who was only seventeen when she decided to give acting a try. Within a few years she attracted attention in *Mystic Pizza* and soon after was receiving Oscar nominations for her performances in *Steel Magnolias* and *Pretty Woman*. Since then her movie credits and relationships have kept her consistently in the spotlight.

It was difficult for Roberts to adjust to the demands of fame. Interview requests, the pressure to accept movie offers, and the loss of privacy weighed upon the young actress. Roberts learned to step back, evaluate her life and career, and come to terms with her worth as a person as well as an actress. Deciding it was pointless to strive continually to make others happy, she has come to understand the importance of making her own decisions and reserving some of her energy for herself.

Roberts cannot escape the fact that she is a highly sought-after actress. She is constantly in demand because she has the ability to bring people to the theater and the clout to bring a project to fruition. For all of her confidence as an actress and movie producer, she has an open, vulnerable personality that has enhanced her acting ability but caused her pain in her personal life. She was engaged to actors Dylan McDermott and Kiefer Sutherland, married to and divorced from country singer Lyle Lovett, and ended a four-year relationship with actor Benjamin Bratt. Throughout her career Roberts's romantic life has been played out in the press. Every time she goes on a date it is newsworthy enough to generate a tabloid story or photo.

Julia Roberts's bright smile and talent make her one of the most sought-after actresses in Hollywood today.

Roberts accepts an award at the People's Choice Awards ceremony in January 2000.

To come to terms with a life that is being constantly scrutinized, Roberts looks for something positive in every situation. She does not look upon her miscues at the box office or her broken relationships as mistakes. Rather, she sees them as experiences that have helped her grow and shape her life. Roberts has learned to make decisions and not look back, even when some of her personal and professional choices have been questioned. Roberts claims to have no regrets about some of her choices, but she has rebounded and used the experiences to enrich her life.

Making movies is what makes Roberts happiest. On the set she finds a sense of family and companionship regardless of the state of her private life. Acting can be an exhausting experience for Roberts, as her talent for calling up and exposing her deepest emotions makes some of her roles extremely difficult and draining. However, with the support she receives from cast and crew members she has learned to make a distinction between the feelings of her characters and her own emotions. The fame her career has generated has made her life difficult in some ways, but she loves the movie-making experience.

In *Pretty Woman,* Roberts wobbled unsteadily into the spotlight. A decade later, she strutted confidently in her Oscar-winning performance in *Erin Brockovich.* Roberts has learned to move forward with her life and her career with enough resilience and confidence to become one of the most powerful women in Hollywood.

Chapter 1

Georgia Girl

JULIA FIONA ROBERTS was born into a family of aspiring actors in Atlanta, Georgia, on October 28, 1967. She is the youngest of three children born to Betty and Walter Roberts. Her brother, Eric, is eleven years older than Julia, and her sister, Lisa, is two years older.

The Robertses were not major television or movie stars, but Julia's parents found a way to make a living as actors. In order to practice the craft they loved, Betty and Walter Roberts taught others to act. While running the Actor's and Writer's Workshop in Atlanta, the pair put on plays ranging from comedies to classics, including Shakespeare's *Taming of the Shrew*. The plays did not make the Robertses rich and famous, but they enjoyed their interesting careers.

As a toddler, Julia would watch from her stroller as her parents put on Shakespeare-in-the-park productions and taught acting classes for children. The little girl was a favorite with the children in her parents' classes. Julia was too young to learn about acting from her parents, but she enjoyed being with her family and later recalled feeling content as a preschooler. Her family was together, and this gave her a feeling of security. It was comforting for the young girl to be with her parents, brother, and sister. She was especially close to Lisa, who shared a bedroom with Julia.

Although Julia remembers being happy as a young child, there was tension in the Roberts's home. Her parents would sometimes have loud arguments or disagreements. When her parents would argue, Julia remembers shutting herself away in her bedroom with Lisa. The young girls would have a tea party, coping with the strained family relationships by creating a world in which everything was orderly and comfortable.

The tension in the Roberts's home caused Julia to miss the opportunity to take advantage of the formal acting lessons her parents were giving. When she was four, her parents' marriage ended in

Atlanta, Georgia, is Roberts's birthplace and the site of her first exposure to acting.

divorce. The acting school folded, and her parents took more ordinary jobs. Her mother worked as a secretary, and her father sold
vacuum cleaners. Only Julia's fourteen-year-old brother showed
an avid interest in continuing the family's acting pursuits.

The Roberts children were split up after the divorce. Following
a custody dispute, Julia's brother lived in Atlanta with their father.
Eric did not get along with their mother and, although he loved
them, he was not especially close to his sisters, who were much
younger than he. Julia and her sister lived with their mother in
Smyrna, a suburb of Atlanta with a population of about thirty-three
thousand.

Smyrna Childhood

While she was in elementary and high school, Julia lived with
her mother and sister in an apartment complex in Smyrna. She
adjusted quickly to her family's new lifestyle. She liked playing

with the children who lived in nearby apartments and had fun swimming in the pool at the complex. The family had many pets, and Julia enjoyed taking care of the animals so much that she talked of becoming a veterinarian.

Julia's father, who lived in nearby Atlanta, tried to remain close to his daughters. At a specific time each week, Julia and Lisa talked to him on the telephone, and they visited him every other weekend. Julia felt close to her father and treasured their time together, especially when he read books to her such as *Charlie and the Chocolate Factory*. Although he was no longer working as an acting instructor, his talent came across as he made up a different voice for each character. Her father had a knack for making things fun, a quality Julia would later show that she shared.

The part of Julia's childhood that included her father, friends, and pets was the happy side. However, other aspects of her family life continued to be stressful. After the divorce, Julia's mother married a man named Michael Motes. They had a daughter, Nancy, when Julia was in elementary school. Julia loved the little girl. The three sisters got along, but Julia didn't get along well with her stepfather, who could be bitter and difficult. He and her mother eventually divorced.

Losing Her Father

More difficult times were ahead for Julia. When she was ten, her father died of cancer. The pain of the loss was compounded for Julia because family members had not told her he was sick. They did not want to burden the young girl with concerns about his health, so his death came as a shock. When Julia was told her father had died, she felt sad, confused, and angry. She was especially troubled by the fact that because no one had told her about his illness, she had been unable to say good-bye to him.

Her father's death changed Julia's outlook on life. Any innocent illusions she had about the simplicity of life evaporated, as she now knew how painful and confusing it could be. "I think when you lose a parent as a young person, it takes away that dreamy quality of life that kids should be allowed,"[1] she said.

Julia leaned on her sister for support and coped day by day with this sudden change in her life. Eventually, she came to accept her father's death. She viewed it as "a happening" that altered her life but did not crush her spirit. "I just figure you're given the cards you're dealt and you act accordingly,"[2] she said.

As an adult, Roberts warmly remembers her father. His death left a void in her life, but she is comforted by the fact that she still feels he is with her in some way. She finds a measure of solace in the belief that he can hear her at any hour of the day when she needs to vent her problems and frustrations.

Average Student

As a child Julia had to cope with many challenging situations at home, but at school she had few problems. She was a normal, average student in the classroom. She had friends, and although she would one day be cast as the *Pretty Woman,* she did not stand out as a beauty among her peers. The grin that would become her trademark was flawed, and she wore a retainer to close the gap in her front teeth. Julia did not worry about her looks, however. She just enjoyed being a kid.

Known as Julie in middle school, she showed a glimmer of performing ability by winning a speaking contest sponsored by the Optimist Club when she was in eighth grade. However, she did not express an interest in acting because she did not want to look like she was copying the acting interests of her parents, brother, and sister. She wanted to establish her own identity and be seen as an individual with her own likes and dislikes. She talked about becoming a veterinarian and kept her acting aspirations to herself. "I didn't want it to seem like I was doing it just because the others were,"[3] she said. When she was alone, however, she thought about becoming an actress. Sitting in the bathtub, she would imagine she had won an Academy Award and was being interviewed at the Oscars by talk show host Mike Douglas.

High School

By this time the family already boasted one professional actor. Julia's brother had left Atlanta for acting school and in 1978 had made his film debut in *King of the Gypsies*. He received a Golden Globe nomination for his performance in the movie the following year. Although her brother was achieving national acclaim for his performances, and her older sister also expressed an interest in acting, Julia continued to bury any inclinations she had toward acting. In high school her only performance was in her

Eric Roberts

Julia Roberts's older brother, Eric Anthony Roberts, was the first of the Roberts children to take to the stage. At age five he began taking parts in plays produced by the family. His interest in acting stemmed from a severe stuttering problem that his father helped him overcome by enrolling him in the family's acting workshop. When Eric memorized his lines, he did not stutter.

After Betty and Walter Roberts divorced when Eric was fourteen, he lived with his father in Atlanta. Still interested in becoming an actor, he had more formal training than Julia. When he was sixteen he left Georgia for the Royal Academy of Dramatic Arts in London. He then attended the American Academy of Dramatic Arts in New York and acted on the stage before turning to movies.

Eric made his film debut in 1978 in the movie *King of the Gypsies* and received a Golden Globe nomination for his performance. His career was halted for a time when in 1981 he was in a serious car accident. He was in a coma for three days, and his face was scarred from the accident.

When he returned to work, Eric was nominated for a Golden Globe award in 1984 for his performance in *Star 80*, a movie about the death of *Playboy* model Dorothy Stratten. His role as the jealous ex-husband who murdered Stratten was so believable that he was called upon to play similar characters many times in his career. In 1985 Eric received Academy Award and Golden Globe nominations for his supporting role in *Runaway Train*.

Eric has been lauded for his method acting and ability to do interesting things with his roles, but his off-screen decisions have caused problems. Frustrated by his inability to turn out successful movies consistently, he decided to go after quantity rather than quality and appeared in dozens of movies, television shows, and miniseries, usually playing a seedy, often psychotic character. Eric admits that problems with drugs and run-ins with the law also contributed to his waning career.

Although he helped his sister early in her career, they are now estranged. Eric has not gotten along well with his mother since his parents divorced, and this has chilled his relationship with Julia.

civics class, when she took on the role of Elizabeth Dole in a mock election campaign.

Although she did not participate in school theater productions, her intuitive acting talent made itself apparent when she wanted to have fun. If she found a class to be uninteresting, Roberts would use her outgoing charm to manipulate the situation. "When we got bored, Jules could be real creative," said friend Joan Raley. "She could muster up tears in a second to get out of homeroom, and I'd have to follow her out to help her."[4]

Julia was not afraid to call attention to herself. When she thought something was funny, everyone knew it. Her hyena-like laugh was so loud the class would have to stop until she got herself back under control. Her English teacher remembers that Julia usually got away with more than other kids in the class. "I was usually very strict, but she would give me that smile and start talking about who knows what, and then we'd all be off the subject. The class would love it,"[5] David Boyd said.

Although she was outgoing and independent, Julia did not see herself as a popular student. She felt that her classmates considered her to be an ordinary average person with little to make her stand out among her peers. She had a group of close friends but was not a top student, great athlete, or polished speaker. She did not think she was especially good-looking and was surprised when she was selected as a finalist in the Miss Panthera beauty contest. She also remembers being the last person in her group of friends to be kissed.

When Julia thought about life after high school, however, a routine career did not appeal to her. She was looking for something out of the ordinary, finally admitting to herself and others that the most interesting career she could think of was to be an actress. Her quiet interest in acting had been piqued when she saw the 1964 film *Becket* while she was in high school. The drama, starring Richard Burton and Peter O'Toole, made her aware of the power of performance. "The whole experience blew my mind," she said. "It was the first time that I was aware of really good acting. And something kind of clicked in me at that moment in time. It really had a profound effect."[6] As high school graduation neared, the prospect of an interesting acting career outweighed any fears

Becket

The film *Becket* that so moved Julia Roberts was based on a play by Jean Anouilh, which in turn was based on the true story of Saint Thomas à Becket, an archbishop of Canterbury. The real Becket was a friend of King Henry II in twelfth-century England. He lived a luxurious life until he was named archbishop in 1162 and renounced his expensive lifestyle. His subsequent opposition to the king led to four knights murdering him in the cathedral at Canterbury on December 29, 1170.

The play and movie explore the depths of the friendship between Henry II and Becket. In the film version, Peter O'Toole gives a fascinating performance as the scheming, frustrated, and immature Henry II who appoints his friend to the post of archbishop because he thinks that will give him some control over the Church. By contrast, Richard Burton is thoughtful and introspective in his role as Becket, who takes his duty to the Church as seriously as he once did his loyalty to Henry. Their captivating performances enhance an interesting historical drama.

The powerful performances of actors Peter O'Toole (left) and Richard Burton (right) heightened Roberts's interest in acting.

Julia had about losing her individuality by sharing her siblings' professional goals. "There comes a time when you have to own up to what's pulling you,"[7] she said. She decided that a move to New York, where her brother and sister lived, was the best decision she could make for her future. "I had convinced myself that I had three choices: I could get married, I could go to college, or I could move to New York," she said. "Nobody was asking me to get married and I didn't want to go away to school, so I moved."[8]

Budding Actress

Three days after graduating from high school in 1985, Roberts joined her brother and sister in New York. In addition to a desire to try acting, the seventeen-year-old had also moved to the city to be closer to Lisa, who had been her roommate and friend while they were both living at home. The sisters shared an apartment in Greenwich Village and would visit Eric, who lived in an apartment on the Upper West Side.

To support herself Roberts worked at a shoe store. The slender five-foot-nine-inch beauty signed with Click, a big-time modeling agency, but did not get any modeling jobs. She looked great and was very photogenic, but she was not comfortable with her looks and did not want to put her energy into modeling. She decided she would rather pursue an acting career while working at the shoe store to make ends meet.

At first Roberts thought the way to become an actress was to take acting classes. She enrolled in a couple of classes, but found they were not what she was looking for. The acting method the instructors employed seemed silly and overdone. When the instructor told students how to use their eyes when they acted, Roberts thought it just made the students too aware of their eyes. Not feeling that she was learning anything useful from the classes, Roberts did not complete them. She had her own ideas about how to convey emotion in a scene and felt strongly that her instinctive acting method was right for her. She decided it would be best for her to follow her own intuition rather than the direction she was given in her classes.

Early Success

After spending a year going to auditions and receiving encouragement but no parts, Roberts got her first break from her brother, whose connections in show business gave his younger sister's career the boost it needed. He was filming a drama called *Blood Red* and knew the director was looking for someone to play his sister in the movie. He asked director Peter Masterson if his real-life sister Julia could have the role. The director agreed, and Roberts had her first part in a movie. She did not have any professional acting experience, but was confident she could pull it off. In the movie she was onscreen quite a bit and got the chance to utter her first line as a professional actress.

A Greenwich Village apartment. After high school, Roberts moved to New York where she shared an apartment with her sister, Lisa.

Roberts's brother Eric (pictured) helped her get a role in the film, Blood
Red, *where they shared the screen and played the roles of brother and sister.*

It was not a big part, but it allowed Roberts to put her first film
on her acting résumé.

The movie was not released for several years, however.
Roberts's next break came later that year when she was walk-
ing down a New York street with a friend. The friend ran into
an agent she knew, and the agent became interested in Roberts.

The agent helped her land the part of a fifteen-year-old rape victim in an episode of the NBC-TV series *Crime Story*.

Playing a girl who had been raped by her stepfather seemed like a very complex role, and Roberts was nervous. She felt she might have gotten in over her head and was not certain how to convey the character's emotions. Feeling confused and over-whelmed about acting in her first television show, she realized that she could channel those emotions into her portrayal of her character. She used her fears about acting to convey the anxiety of the rape victim she portrayed. She was happy with her performance and proud of herself for pulling it off.

Satisfaction

Roberts was not quite as proud of her next performance. As a bassist in a girl-dominated rock band in the 1988 movie *Satisfaction*, which featured Justine Bateman and Liam Neeson, Roberts worked hard on her part and even learned to play bass guitar for her role. She thought she had done a plausible job of portraying her boy-crazy character, but after she saw her performance on screen, the mediocre movie made her cringe. She had delivered several unintelligible lines, slouched her way through a formal party, and uttered lines such as, "How am I going to sing in this steam bucket anyway? My hair is beginning to frizz."[9] Part movie, part extended video for the MTV generation, the band's poor versions of the hits "I Can't Get No Satisfaction," "Knock on Wood," and "Lies (Are Breaking My Heart)" only added to her embarrassment when she saw the movie. The plot included standard teen movie cliches such as a rich boy–poor girl romance, a superficial look at drug addiction, and a protagonist who forgoes a solo career for the good of the group. Roberts turned to her brother for help in getting over her embarrassment at having a role in the poorly received film. They saw the movie together, laughed at how bad it was, and talked over her feelings about her performance and how she could do better next time.

In addition to teaching her how to learn from her mistakes, the movie also introduced Roberts to Neeson, the first of her

The cast of Satisfaction. *In the film, Roberts (standing right) played a boy-crazy rocker.*

famous boyfriends. Neeson played Bateman's love interest in the movie, but it was he and Roberts who clicked offscreen. Neeson, who was fifteen years older than Roberts, had made his movie debut in the 1981 film *Excalibur* and had received some acclaim for his performance as a Vietnam veteran in the

1987 movie *Suspect*. The Irish actor had a reputation as a ladies man and had dated such notables as Barbra Streisand and Brooke Shields. He and Roberts were together until 1989 and lived for a time in Venice, California. Their relationship garnered little attention from the press. Roberts was not yet well known enough to generate media interest, and although Neeson had four movies released in 1988, they were not well received.

Mystic Pizza

Although *Satisfaction* did little for Roberts's reputation as an actress, she continued to go to auditions. She landed roles in the HBO movie *Baja Oklahoma* and on the television series *Miami Vice*. However, it would not be long before the public and press began to take notice of the blossoming young actress. Roberts was slowly and steadily building an acting résumé when she was sent a script for the movie *Mystic Pizza*, a film about three waitresses who worked in a pizza parlor in Connecticut. Roberts assumed she would be auditioning for the part of cute, perky Jojo when she read the script. She did not think she was voluptuous enough to be considered for the role of Daisy, who was described in the script as "the kind of girl men would kill for."[10]

To her surprise, Roberts was asked to read for the role of sexy Daisy. Her first audition for the part went well, but the director did not think Roberts looked ethnic enough to play a character of Portuguese descent. Roberts was not about to let this keep her from getting the role. When she came back for another audition the next day, Roberts had used black mousse to color her hair so that she looked more like the character.

She psyched herself up before going in to do the second reading. Sitting in a room filled with other women auditioning for the part, Roberts listened to the song "Wild Thing" on her headphones to get herself into character and give herself the edge over the other actresses. "I played it over and over again, and the more I played it, the more cocky I got,"[11] she said. The producers took notice. From the moment she walked into the

Liam Neeson shared the screen with Roberts in the movie Satisfaction. *The couple also shared an offscreen romance.*

audition, her boldness made her stand out from the other actresses.

The outgoing, vivacious side of Roberts's personality that had caught the attention of *Mystic Pizza*'s producers also captivated the crew on the set. One day costar Adam Stork heard laughter and saw Roberts sitting on the steps of a house with fifteen crew members around her, cracking up. It was clear that she was comfortable being the center of attention offscreen as well as on.

Roberts's personality did not always endear her to people, however. When she disagreed with a person's actions, she had no qualms about letting her feelings be known. While giving an interview with her *Mystic Pizza* costars at a New York City pizza parlor, she came to the defense of her costar, Annabeth Gish, when a customer sitting in an adjoining booth complained that Gish was bothering him by flicking her hair. Roberts loudly yelled good-bye when the man left and then shook her long hair in his direction. He came back and gestured at Roberts so angrily that she thought he was going to kick her. The man refrained from making physical contact,

Roberts consoles costar Annabeth Gish in a scene from the movie Mystic Pizza.

but Roberts said if he would have struck her she would have had no qualms about retaliating.

Roberts could be both charming and tough, and her ability to bring out these characteristics onscreen was beginning to garner her some attention. Supported by her brother and sister, she was enjoying the beginning of a promising career. Only a few years removed from high school, she was already winning roles and impressing critics. The next steps, however, would take her higher and tax her more than she could imagine.

Chapter 2

Suddenly a Superstar

Roberts's performance in *Mystic Pizza* proved to be a breakthrough in her career. Portraying a tough talker with a tender heart, she pulled off a compelling performance in a movie that received more critical acclaim than had been expected. The suddenness of her success surprised and frightened the twenty-one-year-old. She was driven to become a better actress but was caught off guard by the attention and demands her success was bringing. Her career was becoming all consuming, and she struggled to deal with everything that was required of her.

Roberts could be outspoken and glib, but she also had an inner insecurity about her acting ability. She was being chosen for bigger projects but was uncertain if her self-taught acting style could keep up with the demands being placed on her talent. Roberts needed reassurance and found it on the set of her next movie, *Steel Magnolias.*

Emotional Role

Impressed by her performance in *Mystic Pizza,* director Herbert Ross chose Roberts for a pivotal role in *Steel Magnolias.* In her most difficult part to date, Roberts portrays Shelby, a young diabetic woman who is determined to have a child even though it weakens her health. The role was all the more heart-wrenching for Roberts because it was based on the life of the screenwriter's sister, who died at age thirty-two from diabetes. Although she became friends with the writer's family, she found it difficult to even look at pictures of the woman her part was based on. When she did, she broke down in tears.

Roberts's acting style is to get completely into character, to feel with every breath the same emotions her character feels. Mingling Shelby's feelings with her own, Roberts showed her vulnerability and the depth of her acting talent. In one scene she is giddily describing her pink wedding decorations and trading cutting remarks with her onscreen mother, Sally Field. In the next scene she is in the midst of a diabetic seizure, shaking, pulling her hair, spitting out juice, and crying. The emotional experience was so intense that Roberts needed to be picked up and helped back to her trailer after every take so she could recover.

Roberts's role as Shelby also called for her to portray fear, confidence, determination, and love. The entire film was a challenge for her, but the scene that scared her most was the one in which Dylan McDermott, who played her husband in the film, sneaks

The stars of Steel Magnolias: *(top row, left to right) Dolly Parton, Sally Field, and Darryl Hannah; (bottom row, left to right) Shirley MacLaine, Olympia Dukakis, and Julia Roberts.*

into the bathroom on their wedding day as Shelby is in the tub. Hesitant to share this intimate moment with the world, Roberts was extremely nervous about filming the scene. However, her hesitation only enhanced her performance. She mingles shyness with confidence and gives McDermott a heart-melting look and smile that wordlessly express her character's deep feelings of love.

Support on the Set

Making *Steel Magnolias* was a draining experience for Roberts, but it was the only way she knew how to do her best work. To help her pull off the challenging role, Roberts got support from her costars, although initially she had been intimidated by the experienced actresses. Field had won two Oscars and had been acting since she was a teenager. The cast also included Oscar winners Shirley MacLaine and Olympia Dukakis, a veteran stage actress. Dolly Parton was a popular country singer and actress, and Daryl Hannah had made the hit movies *Splash* and *Roxanne*. Roberts, just twenty-one years old, was the inexperienced newcomer of the group. "The first day it was a little shocking to be in the same room with all those (Academy Award–winning) women," Roberts said. "I wanted to take notes. But they were so down-to-earth. I felt I could go to them and they helped me a lot."[12]

Roberts became especially close to Field, who became like a mother to her. Field invited Roberts over to her house for dinner and to practice the next day's lines. She taught her how to do needlepoint to calm her nerves. The support she got from Field surprised and comforted Roberts, who came to view the cast as an extension of her family. "Sally's inexhaustible support staggered me," Roberts said. "It got so I didn't call my real mother for three months! I would call Sally and say, 'Momma,' and she would just answer me back."[13]

Putting so much emotional energy into the film blurred the line between Roberts's real feelings and those she created for the movie. She carried her character's emotions into her personal life and began an offscreen romance with McDermott. The feeling was mutual, and before long he and Roberts were engaged. However, their relationship couldn't survive the pressures

Roberts and Steel Magnolias *costar Dylan McDermott (left) began a real-life romance during filming of the movie.*

Roberts's burgeoning career was placing on her. Before *Steel Magnolias* was released in fall 1989, their romance had ended.

Hectic Schedule

Five years after she decided to become an actress, Roberts was turning down more movie offers than she thought she would get in a lifetime. After making *Steel Magnolias,* she moved on to *Pretty Woman* and then *Flatliners.* She also made publicity appearances as each film was released. While making *Flatliners* in fall 1989, she filmed until 5 A.M. and then flew from Chicago to New York to appear on television and do interviews with the print media to coincide with the release of *Steel Magnolias.* "I got on a plane, came to New York, did Donahue, Oprah, and Letterman, went home and became dust,"[14] she said.

Pretty Woman

Following *Steel Magnolias,* Roberts took on another taxing role, that of prostitute Vivian Ward in *Pretty Woman.* Acting opposite Richard Gere, Roberts plays a young hooker who agrees to pose as tycoon Gere's girlfriend for a week in exchange for three thousand dollars. The role of a streetwise prostitute was the opposite of sweet innocent Shelby, although both characters shared an inner goodness.

The part of Vivian called for Roberts to deliver both light comedy and serious drama. In a scene early in the movie, her demeanor displays both self-consciousness and sassiness as her sleazy attire shocks the upper-crust patrons at an exclusive hotel. She adeptly banters with Gere as they bargain over her price, but she also shows her character's sensitivity by falling apart when they argue and Gere calls her a hooker. The movie also contains a difficult scene in which her character is hit, verbally abused, and almost raped by a sleazy lawyer, played by Jason Alexander.

Roberts's acting method of getting into her character's emotions made her days on the set exhausting. She needed to be reassured that she was doing well, so Gere would sometimes call her after a day's work and leave positive messages on her answering

Richard Gere sweeps Roberts off her feet in a scene from the 1990 box office hit Pretty Woman.

The Evolution of *Pretty Woman*

Pretty Woman was not originally intended to be the Cinderella story of a hooker and wealthy businessman who fall in love. When Julia Roberts was first cast in the film it was called *3000,* the prostitute's price for a week of work, and offered a much darker, more realistic look at the life of a prostitute. It did not have a happy ending.

However, when the deal for the original movie did not work out, Disney took over the project and altered everything. The studio changed the title, added light humor and a fairy-tale quality to it, and gave the movie a happy ending. Roberts had to decide if she liked these changes, and then she had to try out for the part again. After meeting with director Garry Marshall, she won the role for a second time.

In a way it was a relief to her that the script had been bought by Disney. Now it was easier for her to let her mother know she would be playing the part of a prostitute. "I called her at work," Roberts told *Rolling Stone* magazine in 1990, "and it was like, 'Hi Mom, I got a job.' She said, 'You did? What'd you get?' And I said, 'Oh, it's a Disney movie! I gotta go, I'll talk to you later. . . .'"

Roberts relies on director Garry Marshall for guidance and emotional support while shooting scenes from the film Pretty Woman.

machine. After doing romantic scenes with Gere and getting to know him on the set, it was especially painful for her to do the scenes in which he yelled at her. After each take, she would be sobbing and so upset that she needed to be held by director Garry Marshall.

Marshall had chosen Roberts for the part because she had a "kind of street urchin behavior that disappeared when she broke into that smile,"[15] he said. He was patient and caring with her, coaxing her to walk and act more like a hooker and less like the dignified Southern lady she had portrayed in *Steel Magnolias*. Under his direction her natural talent was molded into a saucily compelling performance.

Showing the same self-confidence she had demonstrated when she dropped out of her acting classes, Roberts also added her own ideas to her character's personality. She had talked to real-life prostitutes while researching her role and had some strong opinions about how she thought her character would react in certain scenes. Roberts was adamant about being true to herself and her character and was not about to let her performance be anything less than something she could be proud of.

The result was a critically acclaimed love story. *Pretty Woman* opened to rave reviews in spring 1990 as twenty-two-year-old Roberts was basking in an Academy Award nomination for best supporting actress for her role in *Steel Magnolias*. She tried to keep her head as her career rocketed skyward. When she received an early morning phone call telling her she had been nominated for an Oscar, she did not internalize what that meant until that afternoon, when she broke down giggling. "It was that kind of feeling of, 'Oh, my God, I can't believe they picked me,'"[16] she said.

But Roberts soon learned that the fame that had come so quickly had a steep price. She could not walk down the street unnoticed. The multitude of offers that poured in put pressure on her to select the best ones. She had to learn to live with the loss of her privacy and an even busier professional life. These outgrowths of her success would continue to perplex and challenge her for years.

Chapter 3

Dealing with Fame

F OLLOWING HER OSCAR nomination, Roberts had to make more decisions about how to allocate her time and direct her career. So many movie offers and interview requests came her way that she was left with little time or energy for herself. For help in keeping herself grounded and dealing with everything that was being asked of her, Roberts looked to actor Kiefer Sutherland. Their relationship, at first, provided Roberts with a caring confidant, but in the end it intensified Roberts's uncomfortable position in the media spotlight.

When Sutherland and Roberts met on the set of *Flatliners* in fall 1989, Sutherland had little idea who Roberts was. He was

Actor Kiefer Sutherland and Roberts became close while working on the 1989 film Flatliners.

not aware of her work in *Mystic Pizza* or *Steel Magnolias,* but he immediately sensed that she had talent. "She was one of the best actors I'd ever worked with," he said. "She was incredibly giving, incredibly open, and she had qualities that you can't even articulate when you're watching her work."[17] His respect for her talent grew to be something more after filming ended.

Sutherland divorced Camelia Kath, his wife of three years, in early 1990, and the twenty-three-year-old actor soon was seen around Hollywood with Roberts. In Sutherland, Roberts found someone who had grown up in show business and could help her cope with her sudden fame. She was aware that many people felt she had no right to complain about her life—she had fame, wealth, a handsome boyfriend, and an interesting career. It helped to have the support of Sutherland, who understood the confines of an acting career and was not judgmental. "If I come home . . . and think my day has been complete garbage, he's gonna listen to that and not gonna say, 'You should be happy,'" she said. "I can have a lousy day. I don't have to be grateful every second. He allows me room to do and feel and be everything."[18]

Sleeping with the Enemy

Sutherland's visits to Roberts on the set of her next picture, *Sleeping with the Enemy,* were a welcome respite from her work on the film in which she plays an abused wife. Her experiences while making *Sleeping with the Enemy* ranged from physically uncomfortable to extremely painful. While filming one scene on a cold night on the South Carolina coast, Roberts was scantily clad and insisted that crew members also take their pants off so they would know just how cold she was. Another scene called for Roberts to fall to the ground and be kicked by costar Patrick Bergin, who played her husband. Roberts wanted to make the fall look realistic, but she tried too hard. Her head hit the marble floor so hard that it bounced, and she ended up with a black eye. Bergin was then supposed to kick a sandbag next to Roberts, but he missed and accidentally kicked his costar in the leg. Scenes like that left Roberts teary and exhausted at the end of the day. She could not leave her feelings behind on the set, and for weeks Roberts was emotionally drained as she played the victim of abuse. Even at home she could not let go of her character's emotional state.

Roberts's energy also was being sapped by her career demands. Although she loved acting, she began to feel as if her fame and workload were taking too much out of her. "I've spent the last year and a half making movies and giving and giving and giving," she said. "But there comes a point where you're losing sleep, and it takes a long time to get anything back from all that giving."[19] Roberts felt empty after losing so much of herself to what she called the "black machinery" of movie-making, which never quit asking her for more. She had fantasies of a simpler life. She yearned to have time to read, garden, or just sit quietly at home, but she was too busy to find time for relaxation.

Roberts wanted to take a vacation from movie-making, but her plans for a break kept getting delayed as she continued to get offers that had to be considered. Taking time off could be risky. If she voluntarily took herself out of the spotlight, the best

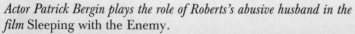

Actor Patrick Bergin plays the role of Roberts's abusive husband in the film Sleeping with the Enemy.

offers would be given to someone else. Roberts could not decide if this was a risk worth taking.

Box Office Blockbuster

While Roberts was making *Sleeping with the Enemy,* her star status was becoming even more pronounced. *Pretty Woman* was released and began an impressive box office showing. Shooting *Sleeping with the Enemy* on location in South Carolina, she was somewhat sheltered from the impact *Pretty Woman* was making on her standing in Hollywood, although her agent frequently called her with updates on her skyrocketing career.

Sutherland was in awe of Roberts and how well she was handling her fame. She tried to keep a level-headed attitude as she became more sought after, and he admired this. "There's a genuine quality to Julia that I don't think is taintable," he said. "She is ecstatic when things are going well and ecstatic when they're not going as well. That blows my mind. I envy it, it's something I aspire to."[20]

Engagement

Roberts and Sutherland tried to elevate their relationship by living together, and he moved into her Los Angeles mansion. Ironically, Roberts was rarely there—she was too busy making movies to spend much time in the home she had bought in January 1990. Despite her busy schedule, she and Sutherland began to plan for the future. He gave her an engagement ring and they planned an elaborate summer wedding. Since they shared the acting profession, they decided to hold the ceremony on a movie sound stage at Twentieth Century Fox. The setting would recreate the mood of *Steel Magnolias* and cost hundreds of thousands of dollars, and the gardenlike set would be accented with trellises and roses. Champagne, beef filets, and a four-tier cake trimmed in violets and seafoam-green ribbons of icing were ordered.

Successful Career, Shaky Relationship

As the wedding preparations were going on, Roberts received more accolades for her professional work. She was nominated for an Oscar for her role in *Pretty Woman,* ranked as the most powerful woman in Hollywood by *Premiere* magazine, and named the star of the year by the National Association of Theatre Owners. She starred in *Dying Young,* due to open in summer, and had been cast as Tinkerbell in *Hook,* directed by Steven Spielberg.

As her career continued to develop, Roberts's personal life became shaky. Her star was rising but Sutherland's was faltering, and their relationship was cracking under the stress of their respective careers. Their relationship and Sutherland's well-publicized night life were the topic of numerous stories in the media as their wedding date drew near. Speculation about the state of their relationship reached a fevered pitch less than a week before the wedding, when Roberts was seen at a trendy spa with Jason Patric, a former costar of Sutherland's and one-time date of Roberts's.

Kiefer Sutherland

By the time Julia Roberts met Kiefer Sutherland on the set of *Flatliners* in 1989, he had appeared in more than a dozen films and television movies. Like Roberts, his parents were actors who divorced when he was a preschooler. His father, Donald Sutherland, appeared in *M*A*S*H* and *Animal House,* and his mother is Canadian actress Shirley Douglas.

Sutherland, who was born on December 21, 1966, spent his early years in Los Angeles where he made his first appearance on the stage at the age of nine. He made his film debut in 1983 in *Max Dugan Returns,* a movie he made with his father. He decided to move away from home soon after making the movie and got his own apartment in Toronto at the age of fifteen. At age seventeen he got his first leading role, in *Bay Boy,* and was nominated for a Genie award for his performance.

In his early career Sutherland played rebels and misfits in movies like *Stand by Me, Young Guns,* and *The Lost Boys.* The cast of *The Lost Boys* also included Jason Patric, who began a romance with Roberts after she and Sutherland called off their wedding. After he and Roberts broke up, Sutherland continued making movies such as *A Few Good Men* in 1992 and *The Three Musketeers* in 1993, and he also dabbled in directing and producing. But his true passion in the mid-1990s was the rodeo. For several years he concentrated on roping and participated in the U.S. Team Roping Championships. Late in the decade he again turned his interest toward acting, and his roles included voice work in the animated movie *Dinosaur.* In 2001 he began working on the television series *24,* in which he plays a counter-terrorism agent.

Campbell Scott and Roberts in a scene from the movie Dying Young, *where Roberts helps Scott cope with terminal illness.*

Wedding Called Off

Shortly before their planned June 14, 1991, wedding, Roberts and Sutherland's relationship abruptly ended. The pair called it off with a joint statement from their publicists stating that "It has been mutually agreed upon that the wedding has been postponed."[21] Distancing themselves from each other both physically and emotionally, Sutherland moved out of Roberts's mansion. She left for Ireland with Patric.

Roberts appeared to be handling the breakup well when she returned to work. In public her demeanor was professional. On the day before she was to have been married, she smiled for promotional pictures on the *Hook* set in Hollywood, happily hugging Spielberg. However, the failed relationship kept her emotions on edge and left her looking drawn. During the filming of *Hook* she thought she heard someone calling to Sutherland on the set and ran for her trailer. She asked that security guards tell him to leave. She was mistaken–Sutherland was not on the set–but her skittish behavior and frail looks concerned her costars, who were not sure that she would be able to deliver a reliable performance.

Months later the mention of Sutherland's name still upset Roberts. When a reporter called her for an interview in November and asked about Sutherland, Roberts chastised him for dredging up painful memories. "You seem to forget that this is my life," she said. "This isn't just a big story for you. I have to live with these emotions you're stirring up here."[22] She hung up the phone, although she called back the next day to apologize and finish the interview.

Jason Patric

Patric was by Roberts's side as she dealt with the couple's decision to call off the wedding. It was at first unclear whether Patric was comforting her as a friend or boyfriend, but the tabloid media was determined to find out. Photographers hid in bushes, surprised them on the street, and waited for them outside restaurants. It soon became clear that the two were more than platonic friends, but it was extremely difficult for them to have their new relationship constantly scrutinized by the press. At first, Patric was determined not to let it bother him. "I've been put under a spotlight not of my own making," he said. "It's hard to deal with it, but I will."[23]

Patric was a shy, private actor who disliked giving interviews. The media attention hit him like a thunderclap. He had made several movies, including *The Lost Boys* with Sutherland, but was a relatively unknown actor until he hooked up with Roberts. Now he could not eat breakfast in public without it turning into a tabloid story.

Although initially he had tried to ignore it, in the end the media attention proved to be too much for their relationship. He had expected it to be difficult, but had not imagined how uneasy the intense attention would make him. "For me, the kind of person I am . . . this was probably the ultimate nightmare," he said. "Relationships, you know, have their own problems, and it didn't help."[24]

Tinkerbell

While Roberts was getting over her broken engagement with Sutherland and sorting through her relationship with Patric, she was making *Hook*, Spielberg's movie about the adult Peter Pan who learns the importance of childhood values. Roberts had gone into the *Hook* shoot thinking that it would be fun to play Tinkerbell in a movie aimed at children. The part was not easy, however. Her role called for her to fly and appear to be seven inches tall, illusions achieved through special effects that required her part to be filmed away from the other actors.

Roberts's scenes were shot on a special effects soundstage that was separate from the one where the film's other stars,

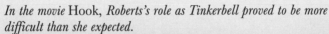

In the movie Hook, *Roberts's role as Tinkerbell proved to be more difficult than she expected.*

Dustin Hoffman and Robin Williams, were shooting their scenes for the $60 million picture. She was placed in a harness and lifted in front of a blue screen. Spielberg read the other actors' parts, and Roberts responded. After her role was shot, it was superimposed over the film footage of the other actors. Some of the shots involving Roberts were technically difficult to set up, taking as long as nine hours to get ready. While the shots were being prepared Roberts bided her time in her trailer on the set. The long waits between shots and lack of interaction with her costars, as well as her personal troubles, made the role an especially challenging one for Roberts.

Although playing Tinkerbell had been difficult, Roberts felt she had done a good job in her role as the lively little fairy. However, the movie was dismissed by critics as being too heavy-handed with its moral that fathers should spend more time with their children. Her light turn as Tinkerbell received some applause from critics but was not enough to counteract the movie's excessive tone. She was also hurt by an interview Spielberg gave to *60 Minutes* in which he hinted that Roberts had been difficult to work with on the set of *Hook*, saying that it had been an unfortunate time for them to work together. He was evasive when asked if he would work with Roberts again. When a reporter asked Roberts to respond to his comments, tears welled up in her eyes. Until she had seen the interview, she had felt that Spielberg had enjoyed working with her. "We did have an enjoyable time," said Roberts, recalling a whipped cream fight on the set with Spielberg. "My only frustrations on that movie at all were that some of the setups took so long. And I didn't quite frankly know what to do with myself all that time sitting in a trailer."[25]

Pulling Back

Coinciding with some difficult times in her personal life, her experience on the set of *Hook* solidified Roberts's decision to spend some time away from acting. Movie sets had previously provided her with a sense of family, but she was now seeing that even the relationships she forged there could bring her pain. Her breakups

Steven Spielberg directed Roberts in Hook.

with Sutherland and Patric, coupled with Spielberg's comments, reinforced her need to take time off. Even before her wedding cancellations and breakup with Patric, Roberts had been planning to take a break from making movies after *Hook*. She had made six films back-to-back and needed to escape from the pressures of her career. It was time to forget movie-making for a while, even though she knew her popularity would be affected by her decision. She needed to take time off to maintain her sanity.

Adding to the pressure of her failed relationships was a downturn in her pull at the box office. *Pretty Woman* had brought in $178 million, but *Dying Young,* released in summer 1991, brought in $33 million. It was still a large number, but low by Roberts's standards.

Painful Stories

Under the glare of flashbulbs, Roberts began to pull back from the media and her work. Throughout her career she had been charmingly and candidly open and honest with the press, but this came at a personal price. She could not deflect reporters' questions without taking every personal query to heart and wondering how her comments would be construed. She was unsure how to deal with fame and the intense scrutiny it brought to her life. Emotionally fragile, she turned down many interview requests and did not take on any new projects.

Roberts was exhausted. She had looked pale and thin after filming *Hook,* and felt she had to make it clear that her demeanor was due to overwork, not substance abuse. She gave a rare interview in November 1991 to refute rumors that she was taking drugs. "I'm scared of drugs," she said. "I'm a big chicken. I have this great energy anyway and I always think that my head would blow off my shoulders or something."[26]

Although she rarely talked to the press, Roberts was stunned at the number of articles written about her and was especially surprised at the media's interest in her romantic life. Photographers sat in their cars outside her house all day, waiting to see if a new boyfriend would visit her home. She did not let their intrusiveness affect the way she went about her everyday life, however. One day she was caught on videotape as she went to get a newspaper, and a newswoman criticized the way her hair looked. Roberts could not believe anyone would think the state of her hair was newsworthy, or that anyone would expect her to fix her hair every time she left her apartment just in case she was being videotaped. She tried to ignore the press and not let the comments bother her.

Working at Relaxing

During her time away from work, Roberts rested and learned how to adjust to a less rigid lifestyle. She could now spend her time as she pleased, but it took her a while to decide how to fill her days. At first she relaxed and enjoyed having the time to do things with her girlfriends. She also took a trip to Costa Rica with

Although relaxing is tough for Roberts, she is seen here spending time with actress Susan Sarandon at a fashion show in 1995.

actress Susan Sarandon. After about a year and a half, she got used to setting her own daily rhythm without having her schedule dictated to her by the constant demands of movie-making. She spent her time just doing what she wanted to do.

During this time Roberts read scripts and considered projects, rejecting all but *The Pelican Brief* and a brief appearance in the 1992 film, *The Player,* in which she poked fun at her own acting. At times she wondered if she was doing the right thing in being so choosy but came to the conclusion that taking a year or two off would not have a big impact on her career. She did not want to accept a role just because she was afraid of being forgotten. She wanted to be in control of her career, not have her career control her. Rejecting scripts she did not like made her feel liberated from the demands of Hollywood. "There were times when I got panicked and thought, Well, jeez, am I ever going to read a good script? Am I being too picky?" she said. "But finally there comes The Calm. . . . Whatever is meant to be will be and will come my way."[27]

Still Popular

Roberts did not need to worry about her status. She had been so popular with fans that Hollywood was happy to wait while she recharged. She was held in such high regard that famed actress Audrey Hepburn chose Roberts to accept an award on her behalf from the Screen Actors Guild and David Letterman gushed over her when she appeared on his show. Although some Hollywood agents and producers feared that it would

Actress Audrey Hepburn chose Roberts to accept an award on her behalf at a Screen Actors Guild awards ceremony.

take her a while to regain her career momentum, others said they were happy to wait.

After almost two years away from making movies, Roberts felt recharged and ready to return to the screen. Taking the time to contemplate her career, life, and stardom led her to the conclusion that she still loved being part of the movie-making process. She had proven to herself that she was a valid person even when she was not constantly working. She felt in control of her life and career and could not imagine doing anything other than making movies. Being on a movie set made her feel part of something larger and more important than herself.

Chapter 4

Marriage and Challenges

Roberts had regrouped and now felt ready to take control of her personal life and her career. As she returned to moviemaking in 1993, she was more conscious of how she wanted to deal with the press. She attempted to control access to her personal life and hoped the media would concentrate more on her career than her romantic life. Although it was news that she was making movies again, and the press duly reported her return to the big screen, her private life became much too interesting for the media to ignore. A secret romance, quickly planned wedding, and unusual marriage only made her personal life more intriguing.

A coincidental turn of events led to Roberts's romance with country singer Lyle Lovett. During her time away from the screen, while hiking through a rain forest in Costa Rica with her friend, Susan Sarandon, Roberts had played balladeer Lovett's music. Sarandon had a roundabout connection to Lovett. Her brother, *St. Petersburg Times* sportswriter Terry Tomalin, had met Lovett at a party for the movie *The Player.* He knew that Lovett carried a video of *Pretty Woman* with him and urged Lovett to call Roberts.

Lovett did, and the interest the two had in each other as artists quickly grew into something deeper. Lovett, thirty-five, was very different from Roberts's past boyfriends. The songwriter and country singer has a quiet introspective personality that is reflected in his melancholy, darkly humorous love songs.

With a weather-beaten face and a thatch of curly hair, he has an odd type of charm. Offbeat but kind, he is a Southern gentleman who offered her stability in contrast to her uncertain hectic profession. He could comfort her vulnerable side and, because he was also in the entertainment profession, could understand some of the pressures Roberts faced.

Secret Romance

Roberts and Lovett began seeing each other in June 1993 but tried to keep their romance from the press. During a press conference at the beginning of shooting for *The Pelican Brief,* Roberts asked reporters to concentrate on her work. However, they persisted in asking her about her relationship with Lovett, although her publicist denied there was anything romantic between them.

Roberts and country singer Lyle Lovett married secretly in Indiana after dating only three weeks.

Rumors about the pair circulated after they were spotted nuzzling and dancing at a café in New Orleans, where Roberts was making *The Pelican Brief.* Lovett also visited her on the movie set. Their relationship was quickly turning serious, and when Roberts could get away from the set she attended Lovett's concerts, watching him from backstage in Tennessee, West Virginia, and New York City. They were secretive about her visits, however. When Roberts visited his concerts, Lovett would dedicate songs to her using "Fiona," Roberts's middle name.

Surprise Wedding

The pair's relationship moved at a rapid pace. After dating for about three weeks, they surprised everyone by getting married at St. James Lutheran Church in Marion, Indiana, on June 27, 1993. The ceremony, which had been planned in less than seventy-two hours, gave Roberts the privacy she craved. Less than two days before the wedding, Roberts had been tight-lipped when a reporter had asked her about her relationship with Lovett. She said little more than that she knew him. The wedding had been planned so quickly that there had been few details for her to hide.

The simple ceremony was in great contrast to the elaborate Hollywood-style wedding Roberts and Sutherland had planned. A barefoot Roberts walked down the aisle in a plain white dress Lovett had chosen. The twenty-five-year-old carried white roses, and Lovett was dressed in a classic black suit. With little time for the couple to extend invitations to the event, the guests were mainly close family members. Among the few celebrities who attended were Sarandon and her companion, Tim Robbins, whose son and daughter were part of the wedding party. Roberts was happy and radiant. Basking in the spontaneity of their romance, she did not want the blissful feeling to end. "I'm afraid I'm going to wake up," Roberts said after the ceremony, "and this will all be just a dream."[28]

Back to Work

The real world intruded on their special day just hours after the ceremony, when Lovett had to get back to work. Marion, a town

Lyle Lovett

Lyle Lovett was a country singer and part-time actor when he married Julia Roberts in 1993. Born on November 1, 1957, he grew up as an only child on the family farm in Klein, Texas. At home he loved riding his motorcycle and playing the guitar.

Lovett studied journalism and German while attending Texas A&M University in College Station, Texas, in the late 1970s. It was there that he found that writing songs was his true passion. He began performing at the age of eighteen, singing at local folk festivals, coffee shops, and clubs. While a graduate student in Germany, Lovett continued to write and perform.

His debut album, *Lyle Lovett,* was released in 1986. Five of the album's singles reached the country Top Forty. He won a Grammy for his 1989 album *Lyle Lovett and His Large Band* and was lauded for the sense of humor he displayed in his songs.

Although he continued touring and writing while married to Roberts, the music he composed and lyrics he wrote during their marriage were not well received. Although he got more publicity than ever because of their high-profile relationship, his 1994 album, *I Love Everybody*, was criticized for sounding stale. After their divorce he returned to his previous form and won a Grammy for the country-flavored album *The Road to Ensenada* in 1996.

Lovett's acting career was launched when director Robert Altman saw him performing at a concert and asked him if he would like to give acting a try. He made his movie debut in Altman's 1992 movie *The Player*. Although he and Roberts both appeared in *The Player* and *Ready to Wear,* the movies did not involve relationships between their characters.

A tireless performer and writer, Lovett almost always uses only his own material on his albums. His eclectic music style incorporates elements of jazz, blues, gospel, pop, and big band sounds, which he blends with his lyrics to communicate a special message with each song.

of thirty-two thousand, had been chosen for the wedding because it was conveniently located between two of Lovett's summer concert tour stops. Lovett had to keep a concert date in Nobelsville, Indiana, that evening.

The newlyweds made the best of the situation, incorporating elements of their happy day into Lovett's show. Wearing her wedding gown, Roberts introduced her husband. He serenaded her with the song "Oh, Pretty Woman," swayed with her to the song, "Stand By Your Man," and gave her a long kiss as the ten thousand fans in the audience cheered. He was eager to share his feelings with his fans. "Welcome to the happiest day of my life,"[29] he told the crowd.

The pair had little time to bask in the euphoria of their wedding day. They had no time for a honeymoon; the day after she was married, Roberts returned to Washington, D.C., where she was filming *The Pelican Brief.* Her coworkers rallied around her, celebrating her new marital status. Crew members showed their support for her marriage by sporting T-shirts that read "Welcome Back, Mrs. Lovett," on the front and "He's a Lovely Boy . . . But You Really Must Do Something About His Hair" on the back.

Although many people wondered what the couple was thinking of by getting married so soon, Roberts had no second thoughts and was proud to call Lovett her husband. She had explained that the wedding had been planned quickly in order to

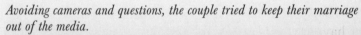

Avoiding cameras and questions, the couple tried to keep their marriage out of the media.

let it be something that was uniquely theirs. They had not wanted to endure the constant speculation about wedding plans from an intrusive press, and they wanted to have a quiet wedding.

However, rather than keeping the press quiet, their marriage only led to speculation about how long it would last. Both were unswerving in the assurance that their love would endure. Lovett said Roberts was unlike anyone he had ever met, and Roberts was confident she had made the right decision by getting married. "I feel liberated in a way," she told *Premiere* magazine. "I feel like this really pleasant calm has descended upon my life. It has to do with your own ability to make a perfectly correct decision."[30]

Energized

Refreshed by her break from movie-making and rejuvenated by her relationship with Lovett, Roberts seemed to have boundless energy. Sharp and witty, she sparred adeptly with the press. When asked whether she ever tired of being called *Pretty Woman,* "Let's get real," she retorted. "Mediocre Girl might have bugged me. Pretty Woman I can live with."[31] She put in twelve- and sixteen-hour workdays but looked vibrant. "I know it sounds like I'm shaving years off my life, but there's a great element of madness when somebody says, 'Action' and you have to do it," she explained. "I remember getting up at seven for school and thinking, 'This is way too early for me.' But man, when that clock goes off, if it's four, if it's five, you get up. There's no 'My stomach hurts.' I sort of thrive on that idea of 'have to.' It has to be done."[32]

Roberts still managed to pull off captivating performances but no longer had to be consoled after each difficult scene. In *The Pelican Brief* she worked especially hard at a scene in which she sees costar Sam Shepard get into a car that explodes. Her face had to convey shock, disbelief, and anguish as her character comprehends what has happened. After filming the scene the first time her eyes were filled with tears, and she was so consumed by the role that she could not speak. Yet director Alan J. Pakula needed her to repeat the scene with a little less

Denzel Washington costarred with Roberts in the 1993 suspense thriller The Pelican Brief.

emotion. She had grown as an actress and was able to pull herself together, containing herself just enough to make the scene work.

Working on Her Marriage

Roberts and Lovett also put energy into making their marriage work. It was not easy with their busy schedules. After *The Pelican Brief,* Roberts was scheduled to make *I Love Trouble* and *Mary Reilly* and had a small role in *Ready to Wear.* Lovett continued touring and admitted that in six months of marriage he and Roberts had not spent more than seven days in a row together. There were rumors that their marriage was faltering, but Roberts insisted that her heart still skipped a beat when she saw her husband and that they talked of having children in a few years. "At thirty, I think I'll feel mature and unselfish enough to take care of children properly," she said. "Too many people have children when they're still kids themselves. Once I learn how to take care of myself and Lyle, then I'll be ready to take care of a family."[33]

Although she was not yet ready to have children, Roberts said marriage made her feel more like an adult. She now had an obligation to consult her husband when it came to making major decisions; however, because of their busy careers it was not always easy for them to communicate. "You should probably tell somebody if you're going to be out until 12 midnight. You should tell somebody that you're spending four months in Australia," she said. "What makes it a little difficult is we go from spending time together to not spending time together. Sometimes he's always there for me to consult, and sometimes it's just me."[34]

The couple managed to inject a few moments of domestic bliss into their marriage. When they were staying together at their rented home in Los Angeles, her Manhattan apartment, or his farmhouse in Klein, Texas, they would have breakfast together, go to work, and talk about their day in the evening. Roberts cooked a big Thanksgiving meal for Lovett and his parents. The pair tried to keep the romance of their relationship alive as well. They snuggled in Paris, and when Lovett appeared at a ski resort in Aspen, Roberts flew there for his concert, and he serenaded her in the empty auditorium before the show.

However, these times of togetherness were rare. Their careers constantly intruded on the couple's time together. Although they were close and affectionate at a midnight supper after Lovett's Aspen concert, Roberts had to fly back to Los Angeles the next day, while Lovett continued touring.

Drifting Apart

The press was only too happy to report incidents that seemed to show cracks forming in the couple's relationship. Less than a year after they were married, Roberts did not wear her wedding ring when she attended a New York fashion show. When Lovett spoke at a tribute to director Robert Altman, Roberts declined to attend the event. A few months later, both were scheduled to film scenes for *Ready to Wear* in Paris on the same day. However, Lovett flew home twelve hours before Roberts arrived. The most publicized incident occurred about ten months after their wedding, when Roberts went out to dinner with actor Ethan Hawke, the handsome star of *Reality Bites,* and others in the entertainment industry. After dining at the Manhattan restaurant they danced together, and Roberts then had to quell rumors of romance. "I love to dance," an edgy Roberts told a reporter as she explained the incident. "And I will continue to dance. I plan on doing as much dancing with as many people as possible. I will dance until I drop."[35]

Roberts and Lovett tried to be realistic about their relationship and make the best of their time together, but sensed they were drifting apart. At a concert in New York Lovett told the audience, "No matter how well you may have planned, things don't always come out as you intended."[36] They tried to pull things back together with a romantic interlude on Valentine's Day in 1995, but when Lovett broke his collarbone in a motorcycle accident in Mexico a few weeks later, Roberts was not

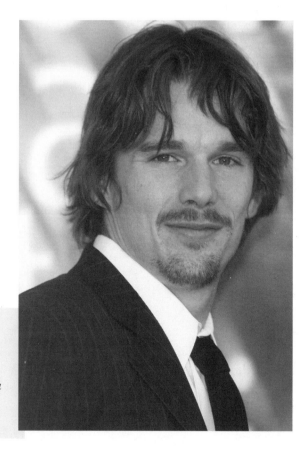

Rumors of a new romance surfaced when Roberts was seen with actor Ethan Hawke at a Manhattan restaurant.

there to comfort him. They announced their separation in late March but said they still were close and supportive of each other.

Tough Times

Roberts buried herself in her work as her marriage came to an end. When the separation was made public, she was in London making *Mary Reilly,* a drama in which she played a maid to Dr. Jeckyl/Mr. Hyde. Wearing dark glasses, a coat, and turtleneck, she left her London hotel and headed to work on the day the separation was announced, while Lovett recuperated from his accident in Houston. Although the separation led to divorce, Roberts and Lovett remain close friends who speak often. She saw their divorce as a difficult but strong decision on their part. "We opted for a real power move, which was the decision to split up," she said. "When people look at relationships, they think that to stay in a relationship, to work on it, is to be strong and to give up on it is really weak. Well, lots of times it's the easy choice to stay. It's the weakness in a person or situation that keeps you together."[37]

It was not easy for Roberts to separate from Lovett and admit that all the reports about their shaky relationship had been true. The breakup taught her she could make it through a difficult time on her own. She now knew she had the strength to deal with her career decisions and life's challenges without needing to lean on anyone for support.

Roberts needed to summon her self-confidence as her career took a dip after her divorce. Although *The Pelican Brief* had been a hit and heralded her comeback to the big screen, the films she made immediately after were not as well received. Competition from *Forrest Gump* and a lack of chemistry with costar Nick Nolte doomed the 1995 movie *I Love Trouble.*

The serious *Mary Reilly* was plagued by production problems. Filming on the picture had begun in spring 1994, and it was not released until February 1996. Roberts had been paid $10 million for her challenging role, which called for her to play a quiet Irish maid drawn to both the good and evil that fight for dominance in Dr. Jeckyl. The tone of the movie was grim and foreboding, and the sets ranged from a creepy laboratory to a gloomy English manor. Roberts hid her good looks behind pale makeup and a flat red wig, a look that required her to spend two hours in makeup each day before filming. The role was rich enough and contained enough subtleties to give her the opportunity to turn it into an Oscar-caliber performance; however, the story lacked a convincing conclusion. Feeling pressured to turn out a film that could justify Roberts's huge paycheck, the movie's director and studio delayed its release seven times, and it opened to poor reviews.

Roberts's decision to tackle a dramatic role in *Mary Reilly* did not bring the result she had hoped for. As she struggled personally and professionally, her star power was dimming. However, rather than feeling overwhelmed by her divorce and poor showings at the box office, Roberts now felt she had the resilience to cope with downturns. She was learning more about the entertainment business and about herself. Responsibility no longer intimidated her, as she was not afraid of making the wrong choices. "There is probably nothing I can't deal with," she said. "Put me in any situation, with any sort of crisis–personal, professional, direct, indirect–that I caused or need to fix, and I can deal with it."[38]

Chapter 5

Trying New Things

AFTER SEVERAL DISAPPOINTING movies and a troubled love life, Roberts wanted to change the way Hollywood looked at her. She did not want to be known only for her flowing hair, glowing smile, and intriguing personal life. Desiring to expand her range as an actress, she took roles that downplayed her looks and challenged her ability. She chose varied parts, edged away from the romance and thrillers that had driven her earlier career, and moved toward more dramatic roles. Her choices were not universally applauded, but at this point in her life Roberts was more interested in growing as an actress and pleasing herself rather than churning out carbon copy hits.

In 1995 Roberts added a new dimension to her standard romantic character in *Something to Talk About* with Dennis Quaid. The movie marked the first film in which Roberts played a mother. Although this movie about a woman whose husband is having an affair received mixed reviews, it proved Roberts's willingness to take on more mature roles.

Roberts tackled a completely different movie genre with a singing part in the Woody Allen musical *Everyone Says I Love You*. Although her singing voice was panned and the quirky film was criticized for a lack of depth, the movie helped Roberts grow as an actress. She showed she was not afraid to jump into a role that required her to try something unusual.

Enjoying Ireland

Roberts could command up to $15 million for a movie, but often took less if she found a part that interested her. For a small role in *Michael Collins,* a 1996 drama about an Irish freedom fighter, she agreed to the paltry (by her standards) salary of about $125,000. She wanted to do the film because the role gave her a chance to unwind in a country she loved and to act in a movie that placed few expectations on her. The movie did not hinge on her delivering a stellar performance, and the lack of pressure was a relief.

Roberts spent four weeks in Ireland while performing her role as the girlfriend of Collins, who was played by her former beau, Liam Neeson. The project gave her a chance to show how far she had come on an emotional level as well. Her romance with Neeson, which had ended eight years earlier, had evolved into friendship.

Roberts enjoyed making the movie so much that she later kept a photo of herself and Neeson, taken on the set, displayed at her home. Roberts wanted to remember her time in Ireland, where she had felt comfortable and the slower pace of life had given her a break from her hectic lifestyle. In Ireland she was reminded that she did not need to race through her life in or-

Roberts and costars Liam Neeson (center) and Aidan Quinn (right) in a scene from the 1996 drama Michael Collins.

der for it to have meaning. She had the luxury of taking things slowly and enjoying the moment, and she found that could be just as fulfilling as working and playing at a frantic pace.

Happy but Hitless

While these roles allowed Roberts to do the job she loved and stretch her acting ability, they did little to bring her a box office hit. Compared to her previous pictures, movies like *Mary Reilly, Michael Collins,* and *Everyone Says I Love You* were box office flops. Roberts also had a small part in the Robert Altman film *Ready to Wear,* a searing look at the world of fashion that was not as popular as it had been expected to be. Although she was only onscreen for seven minutes, some blamed her for the movie's failure. Realizing that many factors beyond her control went into the finished product, she was exasperated when a movie's poor showing was deemed to be her fault.

Roberts tried not to let her struggles at the box office bother her. She was making the movies she wanted to make and was very happy with her work and her decisions. She was determined not to let a fear of failure dictate her choices. "Every time a movie of mine does well, I consider it a blessing," she said. "You've got to. Otherwise you're just asking to be terrorized by the numbers, and I just won't be."[39]

Stars like Sandra Bullock and Julia Ormond were temporarily taking her place as the most sought-after actresses of the moment, but Roberts distanced herself from them as she continued to take on more complex roles. She turned down the leads in *While You Were Sleeping* and *Sleepless in Seattle* because the roles were too similar to what she had done in the past. Not wanting to be typecast as a heroine of romantic comedies, she also decided not to make a sequel to *Pretty Woman.* She probably could have commanded a record salary, but decided she did not want to return to the role that had made her a superstar. She had moved beyond that stage in her life and did not want to recreate the vulnerable sassy spirit she had portrayed so adeptly years earlier. "I just think it was what it was, and to try to make it more than what it was is asking for it,"[40] she said.

*Actress Sandra
Bullock's popularity
rose during a rare
low period for
Roberts.*

Low-Maintenance Life, High-Interest Loves

Roberts was comfortable with the decisions she was making in
her personal life as well. Remaining true to her middle class
roots, she did not feel compelled to look or act like a star.
Preferring dressing down to dressing up, she wore leotards and
sweats when she was not working and did not bother to put on
makeup when she went to the grocery store. She was not ob-
sessed with dieting; she especially enjoyed eating grits and bis-
cuits with gravy but kept her figure slim with jogging and yoga.
Rather than relying on a staff to take care of her housework, she
did her own chores at home. With a low-maintenance lifestyle,
Roberts showed that she did not need to surround herself with a
posse of assistants in order to validate her worth.

Roberts still had a vulnerable side, however, that was pained
by the media's constant intrusion into her private life. She now

had years of experience in dealing with the press, but stories that exaggerated various aspects of her personal life could still wound her. Following her divorce Roberts had to deal with tabloid conjecture linking her to various stars, a bodyguard, and an Italian man she met while making a movie in Venice. She tried to take it lightly, saying it was like reading stories about someone else's life. However, it was difficult for her to brush off her real feelings. She was still stinging from her divorce to Lovett and the fact that the speculation about their shaky relationship had proven to be correct.

When it came to the subject of her former husband, Roberts declined to share details of her breakup with Lovett with reporters,

Julia's Giving Side

Although she does not flaunt her charity work, Julia Roberts has a history of helping. In 1995, a few months after her separation from Lyle Lovett was announced, she visited Haiti for six days as a goodwill ambassador for UNICEF. She toured the country's slums and spent time at orphanages, vaccination clinics, and schools. She has also visited India and Africa to do charity work.

Roberts also makes unscheduled appearances in the United States. When she was in Barstow, California, making *Erin Brockovich* in 1999, she made an unannounced visit to Lenwood Elementary School. The principal had written her a note asking if she would like to visit the school while she was in town, and she surprised him one Monday morning by showing up and spending five hours at the school. She asked that no photos be taken and no autograph requests be made, but she visited twenty-one classes, talking to students about making their dreams come true. At mealtime she even helped hand out lunch.

In 2000 Roberts met Abigail Brodsky, a seven-year-old girl with Rett syndrome. The rare disorder causes a loss of speech and muscle control and occurs primarily in young girls. Roberts narrated a documentary about the disease, *Silent Angels,* and attended a fund-raising event. Abigail later died from the disease, but her fighting spirit made a lasting impression on Roberts, who said she thought of Abigail whenever it seemed her problems were looming too large.

Roberts also helped the city of New York recover from the September 11, 2001, terrorist attack. The New York resident donated $1 million to the American Red Cross Disaster Relief Fund and $1 million to the September 11 Telethon Fund. She also appeared on the fund-raising telethon, saying, "Life is so precious. Please, please let's love one another. Reach out to each other. Be kind to each other."

although she stressed that they remained friends. She regularly sent him roses, and he asked her for opinions on his music. She felt a sisterly type of love for him and said that if he married again she would be very happy for him. "We're friends, so it's not a feud. It's actually ridiculously amicable," she said. "You'd think people who could be that nice to each other could be a couple. But it just sort of wasn't the way it was intended to be."[41] She tried to put a tidy happy ending on their relationship but conceded that it was difficult when she was reminded of him at odd moments. When she heard his music coming out of a store's speaker system, for instance, the emotions his voice triggered, caught her off guard.

The Single Life

Although she was not involved in a serious romantic relationship, Roberts did not isolate herself emotionally. She remained close to her sister and also forged close-knit, family-type relationships with cast and crew members on the sets of her movies. On the set, she was away from the press and did not have to deal with anyone judging how she was living her life or reminding her of her fractured personal relationships. All that mattered was how she was acting that day. "I've always thought of location as an island, where all you have is one another," she said. "It's nice to complete each other for a while and be this big, extended Waltons-type family. A lot of bonding goes on."[42]

Roberts's emotional needs were fulfilled through her family, work, and friends. She enjoyed the freedom that came with being single. In the past she had needed a man in her life to provide her with a sense of security and to comfort her when she was overwhelmed by criticism of her acting and her life choices. Now she had the capacity to cope with difficult times on her own and was having fun flirting and dating.

Roberts was not ready to get involved in a serious romance. In fact, she was so busy and was such a famous figure that she was rarely asked on dates. Some men were intimidated by her star status, others by the media scrutiny a relationship would bring. One who was brave enough to ask her on a date was Matthew Perry of *Friends,* who met Roberts when she was a guest star in an episode of the popular television series. They

Friends' *star Matthew Perry fell for Roberts when she appeared as a guest star on the show.*

first communicated via faxes. He eventually summoned the courage to call her and the poise to speak to her when she answered. She admired his wit enough to have their relationship evolve into several dates. "He's a smart, very funny, talented, handsome man, and he's on my favorite show," she said. "I love being engaged in conversation with this man because he is so terribly clever. Who doesn't like to laugh?"[43]

Their relationship did not evolve into anything serious, however, and neither did Roberts's next relationship with fitness trainer Pat Manocchia. At this stage in her life Roberts was enjoying being single rather than having a steady boyfriend. She would invite her friends to her Manhattan apartment for a home-cooked meal or needlepoint lesson, or spend a night out dancing on the bar at Manhattan hot spot, Hogs and Heifers. Roberts relished her independence.

Value in Mistakes

Roberts learned that she did not have to lean on a man in order to get through difficult times. She could rely on herself and confidently direct her own life. She looked upon her life experiences as lessons and learned from her failed relationships as well as her career decisions. She had not been afraid to try different types of roles, an experience that solidified her belief in herself and took away a fear of failure. A few years of experiments were about to pay off with success at the box office and a satisfying personal relationship.

Chapter 6

Enjoying the Extraordinary

FOR YEARS ROBERTS had been perplexed by how to deal with her fame. Early in her career its demands had controlled her and left her tired and worn out. After a break she returned to the spotlight with the hope that she could keep control of her public image and make intelligent career choices. After finding that she had little control over the outcome of her decisions, she learned to accept whatever happened. She decided to relax and enjoy the life she had with all of its demands and opportunities.

Roberts's self-reliance translated into success as her career and romantic life took an upswing in 1997. After varying her acting repertoire with serious roles and a musical, she was ready to return to the lighthearted romantic comedies that had made her a star. Now her films could reflect the happiness and contentment she felt in her own life.

My Best Friend's Wedding

Roberts was aware that she was giving the public what it wanted to see when she made *My Best Friend's Wedding,* which was closer to the romantic *Pretty Woman* than the dour *Mary Reilly.* In *My Best Friend's Wedding* she played a scheming reporter out to win the affection of her best friend days before he is scheduled to marry another woman.

Although the role was a return to the movie genre that had made her a star, it was still a bit of a risk for Roberts because the sneaky, envious character was not necessarily deserving of the man she was after. Roberts had to make her charming and likable. Roberts did, in a playful, humbling, and bittersweet way. Her smile was back in full force, and Roberts knew that this was the type of role fans wanted her to play. When promoting the film she quipped to a gathering of theater owners, "My hair is a lovely shade of red and very long and curly the way you guys like it," she said. "Please see this movie!"[44]

While the tone of the movie was lighthearted, Roberts did not take the project lightly. As she had done on the sets of her other movies, she worked hard and tried to maintain as much control as she could over the character she portrayed. She expected her coworkers to display the same level of professionalism as she did. "I'm a person who has to express myself, or else I become paralyzed in a working situation," she said. "When you feel utterly disappointed by someone that you have to see every day, you have to tell them."[45]

Roberts, Dermot Mulroney, and Rupert Everett (from left) set a box office record upon the release of the 1996 romantic comedy My Best Friend's Wedding.

Although her days on the set of *Hook* and *Pretty Woman* gave her the reputation of being emotionally fragile, crew members said they were pleasantly surprised by her attitude and found her easy to work with. On the set of *My Best Friend's Wedding*, she grabbed a bullhorn at the end of a day of shooting to say, "Happy birthday!" to a coworker and thank the audience for letting the cast tie up traffic while the movie was shot in Chicago. On and off the set, Roberts eschewed the actions of a prima donna. When she took her dog to be boarded in Chicago while she made the movie, she patiently waited in line with other pet owners. Her coworkers were captivated by her. "Her smile is like a thousand-watt bulb," said Dermot Mulroney, who costarred with Roberts in *Wedding*. "Everybody falls for it, but there's nothing like it when she smiles and laughs. You can't help but be drawn into it."[46]

Roberts was winning people over both in person and in the theater. When *My Best Friend's Wedding* was released in June 1996 it earned $21.7 million during its opening weekend, a record for romantic comedies. The success of the film validated Roberts's belief in the career decisions she had been making.

Conspiracy Theory

Roberts maintained her positive attitude on the set of her next movie, the thriller *Conspiracy Theory*, although her good humor was tested by practical-joking costar Mel Gibson. On the set he surprised her with a gift-wrapped freeze-dried rat. Not to be outdone, Roberts responded in kind by putting plastic wrap around his toilet seat.

Even before she knew about Gibson's practical-joking nature Roberts had reservations about accepting a role in the movie. She had considered rejuvenating on a vacation after making *My Best Friend's Wedding*. She was won over when Gibson, director Richard Donner, and producer Joel Silver wooed her with a brass band while discussing the project with her. They also promised she would have time for a nap during the day.

Roberts ended up enjoying the making of the movie, but the picture failed to live up to the movie industry's expectations.

Although serious scenes filled the screen in Conspiracy Theory, *Mel Gibson and Roberts played practical jokes on each other offscreen.*

The film did all right at the box office on opening weekend, bringing in more than $19 million. However, its gross was $76 million–less than its $80 million budget. The humorous romantic plot was confusing and unbelievable, and the film was a disappointment to Gibson fans who were looking for more of an action-oriented picture. The onscreen pairing of the two superstars had been much anticipated, but the result was not what fans had been expecting.

Stepmom

Roberts's next film, *Stepmom,* was one she had been looking forward to making for years because it paired her with her friend Sarandon. Although Roberts was happy to be working with her friend, she still had occasional feelings of doubt about her own acting ability. On the first day of their rehearsals together Roberts had a moment of panic when she wondered whether her friend would like her acting. However, Sarandon put her mind at ease, admiring her friend's professional attitude toward her work.

In the movie Roberts plays the glamorous girlfriend of Sarandon's ex-husband and is the object of Sarandon's scorn. Some of the scenes made Roberts uncomfortable. The script called for her character to engage in some lively antagonistic exchanges with Sarandon, and these scenes left her feeling down at the end of the day. It had always been difficult for her to do scenes in which her character is chastised by another actor. To hear it coming from her friend made it all the more depressing.

The pair quickly rebuffed rumors that there was any discord between them on the set. The only tension was between their characters. Roberts and Sarandon were happy to be in the same movie at last. It had been difficult for them to find a story with two strong female roles, and when they were offered the script for *Stepmom* they agreed that they liked the storyline. However, it required years of work to get the project from its concept stage to the screen. The script needed intensive reworking and required five rewrites. It took about four years from the time the idea was presented to get the film into theaters.

The movie represented a new level of responsibility for Roberts. She and Sarandon became executive producers on the project, which gave them veto power. Roberts did not find her additional responsibility especially enjoyable. She was not excited when she had to go through version after version of

Although they enjoyed working together, real-life friends Susan Sarandon and Roberts were disappointed by the result of their film Stepmom.

the script. She loved the challenges of being an actress, but executive producer status quickly wore thin. "Before *Stepmom*, if I read a script twice by the time a movie finished shooting, that was pretty impressive," she says. "Though I'm incredibly intrigued by development, it's not my favorite thing in the world. Every time a new version came in, it was like, 'Oh, this again.'"[47]

The resulting movie was less than compelling. Roberts did not even like the name of the movie, saying it sounded too much like a horror film. The finished product was criticized for a lack of chemistry between the stars and a story that did not delve deeply enough into the impact the women's antagonistic relationship had on the children who were involved. Roberts and Sarandon had succeeded in working together, but the result was not what either had hoped for.

Happy at Thirty

While working on *Stepmom* Roberts turned thirty, a milestone that was noted on magazine covers months before her birthday. Initially upset about the attention her age was getting, she came to use the turning point as an opportunity to spend some time reevaluating her life. Her twenties had been fulfilling and educational, and she found value in both the positive and negative things that had happened to her.

Although ruminating about the past decade forced her to deal with issues such as broken engagements, divorce, and the pressures of fame, she had no regrets about how she had lived her life. She was proud of her accomplishments, which were a culmination of the choices she had made. She had such a comfortable feeling about her life that she looked forward to turning thirty. "I began to feel this bliss to the point where I thought if I had known how great thirty was I would have done this when I was twenty-five,"[48] she joked.

Enter Benjamin

Roberts had another reason to feel upbeat at that point in her life. In 1997 she had seen actor Benjamin Bratt dining at a Manhattan restaurant. She was attracted to the handsome star, who played a detective on television's *Law & Order,* and they began dating later that year. His television show and *Stepmom,* the movie she was working on at the time they met, were both being filmed in New York City. After work they would meet for romantic late-night dinners or order Italian take-out and spend cozy evenings at her penthouse.

Bratt was kind, polite, and confident; he had the self-assurance to handle the publicity that came with their relationship. Roberts was drawn to his sense of humor and their similar views on the world. "I realized immediately that he is someone who will always

Benjamin Bratt and Roberts are full of smiles at an awards ceremony in 2000.

challenge me in that great way that keeps you moving forward in your life," she said. "His presence raises the quality of my life."[49] His sense of style and handsome features helped, too. She melted when she stood in front of his sturdy six-foot-two-inch frame. "I felt like Thumbelina,"[50] she said.

Bratt was enamoured of Roberts for the person she was aside from her glamorous job. "Despite all the complexity and chaos that appear to exist in her life, she's also a very simple person," Bratt said. "Simple in the most beautiful ways: generous, soulful, giving, loving—all those things are important to me."[51] Both continued a heavy workload but tried to go no more than three weeks without seeing each other. When they were together, whether at his home in San Francisco or hers in New York, they just enjoyed being part of each other's life. Bratt said most people would be surprised at how normal their lives were. When they left home they were not constantly surrounded by bodyguards. Because they took a low-key approach to appearing in public they could walk down the street in San Francisco or New York without being hounded by fans. They both valued privacy and a peaceful life.

As their relationship lasted months and then years, Roberts continued to be captivated by the giddy feeling of being in love. "We're just ecstatically happy," she told Oprah. "We're drunk with joy twenty-four hours out of the day."[52] They wore matching friendship rings, and whenever Bratt's name was mentioned during an interview Roberts would blush. She gushed about her feelings for him and felt fortunate to have his affection.

Resigned to Publicity

Roberts and Bratt resigned themselves to the fact that their relationship would receive intense press coverage. There were constant rumors that they were getting married or had already wed. The pair tried to treat it lightly, laughing at untrue tabloid stories. Roberts learned to talk with clenched teeth, or not speak at all, when she knew photographers were nearby, so they would not get a photo of her face in a contorted position. The media's determination to capture Roberts on film left her shaken late one night when a group of photographers jumped out of the bushes to take her picture. The incident scared her, but she didn't let it overwhelm her. "Julia's still vulnerable, and she's a sensitive girl," director Marshall commented. "But I think she's learned a lot about handling the life of a star."[53]

Although her relationship with Bratt was duly chronicled by the press, Roberts was savvy in her ability to express, and hide, her feelings about it. She knew how to react when she felt a reporter had gone too far. When Bratt whispered to her as they came down the red carpet at an event, a reporter asked her what he said. She told the reporter that if Bratt had wanted everyone to hear what he had told her, he wouldn't have whispered. "I have more confidence now to speak up and say, 'You are crossing a line'—as opposed to wanting to please other people at any expense to myself,"[54] she said.

Roberts tried to reveal few details about her relationship with Bratt. She dealt with questions about him by telling reporters that she felt he was so wonderful that if she started talking about him she would go on for a week, so it was best for her not to get started on the subject. She also evaded questions about marriage and children, refusing to reveal a timetable for either.

Bratt and Roberts arrive at the Los Angeles premiere of Erin Brockovich.

Relaxing in Taos

Julia Roberts knows that in the midst of her fast-paced life, she needs to have some down time. She has created a sanctuary for herself on a ranch in Taos, New Mexico. At her ranch she finds time to read, rest, play with her seven dogs, ride one of her six horses, plow a field, or plant flowers. She also has high-spirited fun. One time she raced her horse, Cadillac, around plastic barrels with such abandon that she got an egg-shaped bruise on her shin.

Her home in Taos is decorated with photos of family, friends, and coworkers as well as mementos from the movie sets she has worked on. She has plenty of room for entertaining friends, who stay in one of the five smaller houses on the ranch when they visit. Guests can also swim in an indoor pool, play tennis on an outdoor court, or boogie on the dance floor on the edge of a field.

At her Taos ranch she is also sheltered from the Hollywood gossip mill. She gets a weekly paper, but concentrates on her day-to-day life at the ranch rather than what is happening elsewhere. The seclusion and privacy she finds at her ranch makes her time there blissful. "My twenties were pretty much booked," she said. "Now I'm able to realize the luxury that all that hard work can provide me. The luxury of being totally relaxed."

Earlier in her career Roberts had wistfully dreamed of having a simpler lifestyle. Now instead of wishing for a more normal life, she came to the conclusion that the life she was living, filled with movies, scripts, choices, and the constant glare of the media, was normal for her. Instead of fantasizing about a less demanding lifestyle, she enjoyed what she had. Her goal was to entertain movie-goers and give joy to her family and friends. "I find the more normal I make my life, the better it is," she said. "The pressure to do a good job, or to find a script I feel is appealing–those are good pressures."[55]

Notting to Be Ashamed Of

Roberts seemed to be laughing at her own foibles with her next roles, which in some respects mirrored her own life. In *Notting Hill* she played opposite Hugh Grant as the most famous actress in the world. In *Runaway Bride* she again worked with Richard Gere, playing a woman who left men stranded at the altar. The films were both successful, but she denied they were in any way autobiographical. If anything, she said, she had to work hard to keep her own experiences out of her role in *Notting Hill.*

Roberts said she was not trying to make a point by making a movie in which she played a successful actress. She was drawn to it because the movie told a funny, charming, love story, and she wanted to make a nice picture. Although she and her character were both superstars, Roberts pointed out that there were some very big differences between her and her character, Anna Scott. As an example, Roberts pointed to a scene in which Scott refused to have a brownie because she was constantly dieting. "Now you know she's a different person from me, and comes from a different place!" Roberts said. "I think she's most like me at the end of the film. It's then that my character has a stronger sense of what she really wants in her life, and why she wants it, and I just think she's a much clearer person."[56]

Still not satisfied with her ability as an actress, Roberts worked to improve and satisfy the directors she worked with. She did not use her status as an excuse to arrive late or avoid studying her lines. Actress Joan Cusack, who worked with Roberts on *Runaway Bride,* said that the star was, "Really aware—not self-conscious but conscious—of her status. She works hard at her

Roberts plays opposite Richard Gere in the romantic comedy Runaway Bride.

Roberts plays a successful actress with costars Hugh Grant and Emma Chambers in the art-imitates-life film Notting Hill.

job."[57] In *Notting Hill,* Roberts strived to impress director Roger Mitchell, who reminded her to bring her character's emotions, not her own, to the role. In the past it had been difficult for her to separate the two, and in this role her character's life was so similar to her own that it presented Roberts with even more of a challenge. However, she showed that she had become much more adept at dividing her character's feelings from her own. *Notting Hill* producer Duncan Kentworthy was impressed by her ability to be joking around and then suddenly turn serious when it was time to film a scene.

Marshall, who directed Roberts in both *Pretty Woman* and *Runaway Bride,* saw her mature from frightened ingenue to grounded professional. Her maturity did not dim her personality, and she continued to be outgoing, funny, and witty. She remained appealing because although she was beautiful, she was not aloof or exotic but rather a little gawky. "She used to be like a deer caught in the headlights," Marshall said. "Now she handles the pressure. She's matured and is a lot stronger."[58]

Erin Brockovich

After making two successful romantic comedies, Roberts decided to challenge herself again. She elected to star in Steven Soderbergh's *Erin Brockovich,* a suspenseful story of a sexy, crusading mother who uncovers a contaminated water scandal and takes on a huge utility company. It was her first dramatic role in years, yet Roberts knew it was right for her. During the ten-week shoot, something clicked. It was as if she had been on the quest for the perfect picture and had found the ultimate movie-making experience. Roberts said her performance in *Brockovich* had been her best to date because the role "was the most challenging, the most well-rounded, had the widest scope of a person to play."[59]

Roberts used her own experiences to help her deliver a realistic performance in *Brockovich.* Her character knew she was right but faced the seemingly insurmountable task of taking on a huge utility company. Roberts felt the same way when she was hounded by the tabloid media. Both needed resilience to deal with their situation. "I have a strong understanding of the frustration she felt," Roberts said. "She was right and she didn't know how to prove it. And she was not a person anyone would ever assume was right. What she did was extraordinary."[60]

Although she used the parallels between their lives to help her deliver a strong performance, Roberts also managed to lose herself completely in the role when she was onscreen. There was no trace of Roberts's successful romantic comedies in this film. In *Brockovich* she became the earthy crusader and compellingly told her story.

$20 Million Woman

In addition to Roberts's outstanding performance in *Erin Brockovich,* her role was also notable because of the pay she received. Roberts broke through to a new salary level when she received $20 million for making the movie, becoming the first woman to make that much money for a single picture. By commanding that salary, Roberts broke an industry double standard that paid male stars more than female stars. Roberts had made five movies that had

Roberts and Albert Finney star in the film Erin Brockovich.

grossed more than $100 million. Some male stars commanded $20 million after only one such picture. Her long-time agent, Elaine Goldsmith-Thomas, firmly pointed out the discrepancy, and Roberts got the money she deserved. "Julia earned it a long time ago, as far as I'm concerned,"[61] said Universal Studios chairman Stacey Snider.

Roberts, however, was unaffected by her new pay schedule. To her, it was just a number. She would rather be known as a great friend or talented actress than a rich superstar. Roberts did not need a record-setting paycheck to make her feel good about herself and her life. She had already accomplished that. By weaving her experiences into a tapestry of her own design, she created a life that made her stardom bearable. Dividing her time between movie locations and her homes in Taos and New York, she eschewed many of the trappings of celebrity life, avoiding excessive parties and glamorous looks. She continued to dress in sweats, often went without makeup, and did her own cleaning and cooking. She liked to read or watch TV, and when she had to get around New York she often took the bus or subway. Wanting to please only herself, she lived a down-to-earth life, feeling like a pioneer woman when she stayed at her ranch by herself. "I do believe that I have an extraordinary job," she said. "But that doesn't mean that I have an extraordinary life."[62]

Chapter 7

Oscar Winner

Roberts's LIFE TILTED a little more toward the extraordinary when she was nominated for an Academy Award for best actress for her role in *Erin Brockovich*. It was her third nomination, and she tried to remain calm, but could not help feeling excited. She had been nominated twice early in her career, but now knew how difficult awards were to come by.

Roberts learned of her Academy Award nomination when she was on the set of *The Mexican,* a caper movie she was making with Brad Pitt. The cast and Roberts later celebrated her honor in Los Angeles, and she tempered her giddiness by maintaining a stoic exterior. She was thrilled to be nominated, but hesitated to admit how

Roberts (left) and Brad Pitt (third from left) pose with colleagues from the movie The Mexican. *It was during the making of this film that she learned of her Oscar nomination for* Erin Brockovich.

much it meant to her. "Inside, I'm doing cartwheels, upside down, naked," she said. "But outside? Outside, I'm keeping cool."[63]

Exuberant Winner

Roberts was favored to win the award, and before Oscar night picked up a Los Angeles Film Critics Award and Golden Globe for her performance. However, she was still nervous and hesi-

Roberts accepts the Oscar for Best Actress for her extraordinary portrayal of Erin Brockovich.

tated to count on coming home with the prize. She tried to enjoy the weeks leading up to the event. She took a vacation and attempted to relax by visiting friends and spending time with Bratt. When the night of the awards arrived, she attended the ceremony with Bratt, her sister, and brother-in-law and tried not to let her nerves get in the way of a good time. "The four of us just went into the night with such a spirit of fun,"[64] she said.

Roberts got to share her playful attitude with the audience when she won the best actress award. Roberts flashed her trademark smile as she walked to the microphone and gave a witty, babbling, exuberant, acceptance speech in which she thanked family members and coworkers. She knew her speech was taking longer than it was supposed to but told bandleader Bill Conti that he should not be too quick to cut her off with a burst of music because she might never win again. Although she neglected to mention the real Erin Brockovich in her speech, she thanked Brockovich later in backstage interviews, explaining the omission by saying she had been overwhelmed by emotion when she was onstage accepting the award. "It was such an out-of-body experience," she said. "Just the adrenaline alone–I have a new-found respect for anybody who gets up on that stage and shows any kind of poise, because to me it was a physiological impossibility. My heart was pounding like a rabbit's."[65]

The award brought a new level of respect to Roberts's career. She was called the most powerful celebrity on the planet, and *Time* magazine named her America's best movie star. She was heralded for her ability to add a spark to any movie she appeared in as well as keeping the public's interest with a sizzling personal life.

More Comedies

After *Brockovich* Roberts did not feel compelled to take on more serious dramatic roles such as the one that had won her an Oscar. She knew the public liked to see her in lighter parts and returned to making romantic comedies. After *The Mexican,* for which she and Pitt both reduced their usual salaries, she made *America's Sweethearts,* which satirized the public relations spin put on the lives of actors and actresses. Roberts was enjoying the lighter roles after the heavier *Brockovich.* "I just want to play the good parts that come my way," she said. "If I'm trying to avoid anything it's repeating myself."[66]

Although she was aware these movies were not Oscar-caliber material, Roberts continued to impress her costars with her dedication. "There are scenes where she was crying for 16 hours, and she was there each take, working just as hard as the take before, and didn't have to be,"[67] said James Gandolfini, who costarred in *The Mexican* with Roberts. Gore Verbinski, the director of *The*

Benjamin Bratt escorts Oscar-winner Roberts to a post–Academy Awards party.

John Cusack, Catherine Zeta-Jones (center), and Roberts in the movie America's Sweethearts.

Mexican, said he had never met anyone as alive as Roberts, adding that she had only begun to tap her talent.

Hesitating to Marry

Roberts and Bratt tried to work their relationship into their busy movie-making schedules. Between 1999 and 2001 the pair worked on nine movies between them. Their work took them to Los Angeles, Las Vegas, Texas, Montreal, Belize, and Australia. When they were apart they tried to stay in touch, and Roberts even mailed homemade cookies to Bratt while he was making a movie in Belize.

When they were together Roberts and Bratt were open about their affection for each other. They held hands while window shopping, kissed at a café, and strolled together arm in arm. Roberts had acknowledged Bratt in her Golden Globe acceptance speech in early 2001, saying, "It only means something if you have someone to share it with."[68] At a New York gala held in her honor at the American Museum of the Moving Image on March 4, 2001, she had called him "the best reason to go home that I can think of."[69]

Roberts holds the Golden Globe award she won for Best Actress in a drama for her role in Erin Brockovich.

Every accolade and award she received gave Roberts another reason to maintain her busy career and current lifestyle. However, Bratt wanted something else. He hoped Roberts would slow down and commit to marriage, but Roberts was not interested in taking that step. She wanted a simple relationship and was satisfied with cruising along as things were. She had finally reached a comfortable place in her life and was happy with how she had shaped it. Marriage did not fit into her plan.

Roberts had experienced marriage with Lovett and knew the work involved in making a marriage successful. She also knew that she was not ready to scale back her career to give marriage the energy she knew it would require. She felt life was a mixture of choices, compromises, and sacrifices and was not ready to sacrifice her independence for marriage.

Although she and Bratt were very much a couple, they still maintained separate identities. When not on movie locations, Bratt lived in San Francisco while she spent time at her homes in New York and Taos. Roberts viewed marriage as a change that could disrupt her carefully constructed world. Constant questions from the press only added pressure to the couple to make a decision about their relationship. "It's funny how everyone is always waiting for the next step, but they're anticipating it, which kind of ruins it," she said. "Get married, make it tidy, and then we can all anticipate your getting divorced. Too tedious. Where's the pizzazz?"[70]

Breaking Up

Roberts's attachment to her coworkers on movie sets fulfilled her need to be loved and supported. This included having fun with her costars on the sets of *The Mexican* and *Ocean's Eleven,* which starred Brad Pitt, Matt Damon, and George Clooney. "We had a dormitory life going there," said Jerry Weintraub, producer of *Ocean's Eleven.* "We were in each other's rooms constantly, drinking, eating, partying and having a good time."[71] Roberts often spoke of Bratt while on the set, but on some levels her emotional needs were being fulfilled by her work, not her boyfriend. He did not want to accept this arrangement.

The stress of their careers and inability to agree on marriage eventually severed their relationship. In summer 2001 it was announced that Roberts and Bratt were no longer together. Wanting to keep it private, they kept the news hidden from the press for several weeks. Shortly before news of their breakup became public, a reporter asked Roberts about Bratt during promotional interviews for *America's Sweethearts*. She lauded Bratt's integrity, the mutual respect they had in their relationship, and how he had taught her to take comfort in her privacy. But she also added that talking about him made her stomach hurt.

Their relationship had ended when it hit a point where it was not growing any more. Roberts admitted on *The Late Show With David Letterman* that she still loved Bratt even though their relationship did not work out. "He's a good man. He's a fine man. He is, to the exultation of the female single population, not my man anymore,"[72] she said, adding that their breakup was tenderhearted rather than ugly. Friends were surprised by their move. Many had expected the pair to get married. "They were into each other's heads and souls," said Howard Rosenman,

Actor George Clooney and Roberts appear in a scene from the film Ocean's Eleven.

Emma Roberts

Julia Roberts is not close to her brother, Eric, but is a doting aunt to his daughter, Emma. Eric and Emma's mother, Kelly Cunningham, ended their relationship several months after Emma was born, but Roberts remained close to her niece. Roberts has said she does not know when she will have her own children, so she spends as much time as she can with Emma.

Roberts has proven to be a fun aunt. When Emma was eight she visited Roberts's ranch in Taos, New Mexico, and wanted to draw a picture. When she could not find any paper, Roberts let her niece draw a mural on the bathroom wall. Roberts also appreciates Emma's opinion on fashion. When she was deciding what to wear to the Oscars in 2001, Emma helped her select a vintage 1982 Valentino gown.

Emma has inherited the family penchant for acting. When she was four she walked around the house talking in an English accent. She begged her mother to take her to an audition for *Blow*, a 2001 movie starring Johnny Depp, and got the part as Depp's daughter. Director Ted Demme said her tough scenes did not intimidate her. Emma only aspires to act as well as her famous aunt. "I wish I could act as good as her," she said, "but I just do my best."

Roberts's friend. "They were supportive of each other. They looked like they were in love."[73]

Polishing Her Life

Although not every decision has brought her instant happiness, Roberts is pleased with how her life is going and contends that in the long term her choices will prove to be the correct ones. She realizes that her life could use some polishing, but she does not want to make any big changes. As she matures she wants to get better at what she does without changing her core values. She strives to maintain the innocent love of life she had when she first came to New York and temper it with the wisdom that her experiences have added.

Roberts has said she would rather have people attracted to her for the way she participates in life rather than her looks. She feels people are attracted to her because she projects a sense of fun and always looks like she is where she wants to be. She is a vivacious spirit who does not regret how she has lived her life. "I truly believe that I was born with a destiny of joy,"

The 2001 People's Choice Awards honored Roberts as Favorite Motion Picture Actress of 2001.

she said. "And no matter what I do, no matter what any of us do to tamper with our lives, you can't really fight destiny. . . . Even in my lowest moment, my darkest hour, I never have a fear of sadness. In the back of my mind there's that comfort that my heart will rally, regardless. It just will, because it knows no other way."[74]

Notes

Chapter 1: Georgia Girl

1. Quoted in Chris Heath, "Portrait of a Trash-Talking Lady," *Rolling Stone,* April 13, 2000, p. 77.
2. Quoted in Kevin Sessums, "The Crown Julia," *Vanity Fair,* October 1993, p. 234.
3. Quoted in Tom Christie, "Woman of Character," *Vogue,* April 1990, p. 394.
4. Quoted in Susan Schindehette, "The Jewel Who's Julia," *People Weekly,* September 17, 1990, p. 92.
5. Quoted in Alex Tresniowski et al, "Julia Roberts: ACTRESS. (The 50 Most Beautiful People in the World 2000)," *People Weekly,* May 8, 2000, p. 76.
6. Quoted in "Rendezvous with Tim and Julia," *Interview,* January 1995, p. 82.
7. Quoted in Christie, "Woman of Character," *Vogue,* April 1990, p 394.
8. Quoted in Myra Forsberg, "Julia Roberts Faces a Character Test," *New York Times,* March 19, 1990, p. 15.
9. Julia Roberts as Daryle Shane in *Satisfaction,* Twentieth Century Fox, 1988.
10. Quoted in James Kaplan, "A Starlet Is Born," *Rolling Stone,* January 12, 1989, p. 29.
11. Quoted in Kaplan, "A Starlet Is Born," *Rolling Stone,* January 12, 1989, p. 29.

Chapter 2: Suddenly a Superstar

12. Quoted in Nancy Mills, "Woman of Steel: Julia Roberts," *Cosmopolitan,* November 1989, p. 144.

13. Quoted in Jill Rachlin and Jeff Robin, "The *Steel Magnolias* Scrap Book," *Ladies Home Journal*, November 1989, p. 126.

14. Quoted in Brian D. Johnson, "Dolled Up in Dixie," *Maclean's*, November 20, 1989, p. 84.

15. Quoted in Tresniowski et al, "Julia Roberts: ACTRESS," *People Weekly*, May 8, 2000, p. 76.

16. Quoted in Schindehette, "The Jewel Who's Julia," *People Weekly*, September 17, 1990, p. 92.

Chapter 3: Dealing with Fame

17. Quoted in Steve Pond, "Pretty Woman Indeed," *Rolling Stone*, August 9, 1990, p. 50.

18. Quoted in Sally Ogle Davis, "Julia Roberts, Shooting Star," *Ladies Home Journal*, July 1991, p. 96.

19. Quoted in Pond, "Pretty Woman Indeed," *Rolling Stone*, August 9, 1990, p. 50.

20. Quoted in Pond, "Pretty Woman Indeed," *Rolling Stone*, August 9, 1990, p. 50.

21. Quoted in "Calling it Off: Julia Roberts and Kiefer Sutherland Put the Wedding on Hold," *People Weekly*, June 24, 1991, p. 48.

22. Quoted in J. Randy Taraborrelli, "Pretty Strong Woman," *Good Housekeeping*, September 1997, p. 90.

23. Quoted in J.D. Heyman, "Too Good to Be True," *US Weekly*, July 16, 2001, p. 36.

24. Quoted in Jess Cagle, "Jason Unmasked," *Entertainment Weekly*, December 24, 1993, p. 16.

25. Quoted in Sessums, "The Crown Julia," *Vanity Fair*, October 1993, p. 234.

26. Quoted in Sessums, "The Crown Julia," *Vanity Fair*, October 1993, p. 234.

27. Quoted in Sessums, "The Crown Julia," *Vanity Fair*, October 1993, p. 294.

Chapter 4: Marriage and Challenges

28. Quoted in Levitt, "Lovett First Sight," *People Weekly*, July 12, 1993, p. 40.

29. Quoted in Levitt, "Lovett First Sight," *People Weekly*, July 12, 1993, p. 40.

30. Quoted in Karen S. Schneider, "One Last Sad Song," *People Weekly,* April 10, 1995, p. 96.

31. Quoted in "Julia Roberts," *People Weekly,* May 9, 1994, p. 145.

32. Quoted in Mark Harris, "Julia Roberts," *Entertainment Weekly,* June 24, 1994, p. 32.

33. Quoted in Susan Price, "Julia, Her Lessons in Love," *Ladies Home Journal,* June 1994, p. 96.

34. Quoted in David Rensin, "Julia Makes Trouble," *Rolling Stone,* July 14, 1994, p. 56.

35. Quoted in Harris, "Julia Roberts," *Entertainment Weekly,* June 24, 1994, p. 32.

36. Quoted in Schneider, "One Last Sad Song," *People Weekly,* April 10, 1995, p. 96.

37. Quoted in Melina Gerosa, "Truly Julia," *Ladies Home Journal,* September 1995, p. 136.

38. Quoted in Gerosa, "Truly Julia," *Ladies Home Journal,* September 1995, p. 136.

Chapter 5: Trying New Things

39. Quoted in Jeff Giles, "The 20 Million Dollar Woman," *Newsweek,* March 13, 2000, p. 56.

40. Quoted in Jeff Gordinier, "The Next Julia Roberts," *Entertainment Weekly,* August 11, 1995, p. 22.

41. Quoted in Michael Segell, "Julia Roberts: Still Falling in Love with Love," *Cosmopolitan,* July 1996, p. 42.

42. Quoted in Segell, "Julia Roberts: Still Falling in Love with Love," *Cosmopolitan,* July 1996, p. 42.

43. Quoted in Jeff Gordinier, "Living the Life of Reilly," *Entertainment Weekly,* February 23, 1996, p. 22.

Chapter 6: Enjoying the Extraordinary

44. Quoted in Kyle Smith, "A Star Brightens," *People Weekly,* July 7, 1997, p. 70.

45. Quoted in Gordinier, "The Next Julia Roberts," *Entertainment Weekly,* August 11, 1995, p. 22.

46. Quoted in Smith, "A Star Brightens," *People Weekly,* July 7, 1997, p. 70.

47. Quoted in Andrew Essex, "Acting Aces Susan Sarandon and Julia Roberts Go Head-to-Head in the Holiday Family Tearjerker *Stepmom*–and They're Still Speaking!" *Entertainment Weekly,* November 27, 1998, p. 24.

48. Quoted in Melina Gerosa, "Fascinating Talk with Fascinating Women," *Ladies Home Journal,* January 1999, p. 102.

49. Quoted in Liz Smith, "The Joys of Julia," *Good Housekeeping,* August 1999, p. 102.

50. Quoted in Leslie Marshall, "Don't Fence Her In," *In Style,* January 1, 2000, p. 144.

51. Quoted in Karen S. Schneider et al, "Then and Wow!" *People Weekly,* March 20, 2000, p. 100.

52. Quoted in Tresniowski et al, "Julia Roberts: ACTRESS," *People Weekly,* May 8, 2000, p. 76.

53. Quoted in Schneider et al, "Then and Wow!" *People Weekly,* March 20, 2000, p. 100.

54. Quoted in Smith, "The Joys of Julia," *Good Housekeeping,* August 1999, p. 102.

55. Quoted in Bonnie Churchhill, "Just a Normal Girl-Next-Door Superstar," *Christian Science Monitor,* May 28, 1999, p. 19.

56. Quoted in Churchhill, "Just a Normal Girl-Next-Door Superstar," *Christian Science Monitor,* May 28, 1999, p. 19.

57. Quoted in Schneider et all, "Then and Wow!" *People Weekly,* March 20, 2000, p. 100.

58. Quoted in "Julia Roberts," *People Weekly,* May 14, 2001, p. 122.

59. Quoted in Heath, "Portrait of a Trash-Talking Lady," *Rolling Stone,* April 13, 2000, p. 70.

60. Quoted in Marshall Sella, "Julia Tells a Lie," *Harper's Bazaar,* March 2000, p. 362.

61. Quoted in Giles, "The Twenty Million Dollar Woman," *Newsweek,* March 13, 2000, p. 56.

62. Quoted in Marshall, "Don't Fence Her In," *In Style,* January 1, 2000, p. 144.

Chapter 7: Oscar Winner

63. Quoted in Mal Vincent, "*The Mexican* Star Julia Roberts Basks in Her Oscar Nomination," Knight-Ridder/Tribune News Service, February 28, 2001.

64. Quoted in Liz Smith, "Julia Settles In," *Good Housekeeping,* August 2001, p. 100.

65. Quoted in Smith, "Julia Settles In," *Good Housekeeping,* August 2001, p. 100.

66. Quoted in Mike Turner, "Up for an Oscar, Julia Plays it Cool and Pushes Her Newest Film," Knight-Ridder/Tribune News Service, March 2, 2001.

67. Quoted in Juliann Garey, "The Real Julia," *Redbook,* April 2001, p. 128.

68. Quoted in Vincent, "*The Mexican* Star Julia Roberts Basks in Her Oscar Nomination," Knight-Ridder Tribune/News Service, February 28, 2001.

69. Quoted in Heyman, "Too Good to Be True," *Us Weekly,* July 16, 2001, p. 32.

70. Quoted in Marshall, "Ain't Life Grand? Or, Rather, Ain't Her Life Grand?" *In Style,* March 1, 2001, p. 438.

71. Quoted in Anne-Marie O'Neill et al, "Their Separate Ways," *People Weekly,* July 16, 2001, p. 72.

72. Quoted in Leo Standora, "Julia Roberts Tells Letterman She Still Loves Bratt," Knight-Ridder/Tribune News Service, July 10, 2001.

73. Quoted in O'Neill et al, "Their Separate Ways," *People Weekly,* July 16, 2001, p. 72.

74. Quoted in Marshall, "Ain't Life Grand? Or Rather, Ain't Her Life Grand?" *In Style,* March 1, 2001, p. 438.

Important Dates in the Life of Julia Roberts

1967
Julia Fiona Roberts is born on October 28, 1967, in Atlanta, Georgia.

1985
Roberts graduates from high school and leaves Smyrna, Georgia, to live with her sister and try acting in New York City.

1986
Roberts gets her first break when her brother helps her land a small part in the drama *Blood Red;* however, the movie isn't released until 1990.

1988
Roberts makes her first appearances on the big screen in *Mystic Pizza* and *Satisfaction.*

1989
A moving performance as a dying mother in *Steel Magnolias* earns Roberts her first Oscar nomination.

1990
Roberts's superstar status is sealed with her performance in the blockbuster hit *Pretty Woman,* for which she earns her second Academy Award nomination.

1991
After her wedding to Kiefer Sutherland is cancelled days before the scheduled event, Roberts leaves for Ireland with new beau Jason Patric; she appears in *Sleeping with the Enemy, Dying Young,* and *Hook* and decides to take a break from her busy schedule.

1992
Roberts relaxes and reflects on her life and star status; she makes a brief onscreen appearance in *The Player.*

1993
Roberts returns to movie-making with the hit *The Pelican Brief;* she surprises friends and fans by marrying country music singer Lyle Lovett on June 27, 1993, after a three-week courtship.

1994
A starring role in *I Love Trouble* and brief appearance in *Ready to Wear* mark the beginning of a box-office slump for Roberts.

1995
Roberts continues to stretch her talent by taking on the role of a mother in *Something to Talk About,* but the movie isn't a critical success; her marriage to Lovett ends in divorce.

1996
Serious parts in *Mary Reilly* and *Michael Collins* and a role in the Woody Allen musical *Everyone Says I Love You,* which calls for her to sing, help Roberts grow as an actress but do little to bring fans to the theater.

1997
The romantic comedy *My Best Friend's Wedding* rejuvenates Roberts's status at the box office; she makes *Conspiracy Theory* with Mel Gibson; her personal life gets a boost when she meets actor Benjamin Bratt and they begin a multi-year relationship.

1998
Roberts takes on the role of executive producer in addition to starring in *Stepmom* with her friend Susan Sarandon.

1999
Giving fans what they want, Roberts makes the romantic comedies *Notting Hill* and *Runaway Bride.*

2000
Roberts again gives drama a try and this time hits it big with her performance as tough sassy *Erin Brockovich;* she earns her first Academy Award for her performance.

2001
Roberts follows her Oscar-winning performance with lighter roles in *The Mexican, America's Sweethearts,* and *Ocean's Eleven;* she is on her own again after her relationship with Bratt dissolves.

For Further Reading

Books

Rosemary Wallner, *Julia Roberts*. Minneapolis, MN: Abdo and Daughters, 1991. A brief look at Roberts's early career.

Wayne Wilson, *Julia Roberts*. Bear, DE: Mitchell Lane, 2001. A concise overview of the actress's career.

Periodicals

Jess Cagle, "Julia Roberts: Great Looks, Box-Office Clout, Oscar-Certified Talent and a Tempestuous Love Life Make Her the Reigning Queen of Hollywood," *Time,* July 9, 2001.

Richard Corliss, "What Makes Her the Best," *Time,* July 9, 2001.

Chris Heath, "Portrait of a Trash-Talking Lady," *Rolling Stone,* April 13, 2000.

J.D. Heyman, "Too Good to Be True," *US Weekly,* July 16, 2001.

Nancy Mills, "Woman of Steel: Julia Roberts," *Cosmopolitan,* November 1989.

Susan Schindehette, "The Jewel Who's Julia," *People Weekly,* September 17, 1990.

Karen S. Schneider, "One Last Sad Song," *People Weekly,* April 10, 1995.

Websites

Abcnews.com (www.abcnews.go.com/sections/entertainment). Search for Julia Roberts to find the latest showbiz news about her.

The Movie Times (www.the-movie-times.com/thrsdir/actress/jroberts.html). A good source for box office statistics, message boards, and photos. It also gives fans the opportunity to buy her movies.

People.com (www.people.com). Facts, news, features, and career highlights for Roberts and other celebrities.

Works Consulted

Periodicals

David Ansen, *My Best Friend's Wedding,* reviewed in *Newsweek,* June 23, 1997.

Tim Appelo, "Partners in Crime," *Entertainment Weekly,* November 22, 1996.

Jess Cagle, "Jason Unmasked," *Entertainment Weekly,* December 24, 1993.

Tom Christie, "Woman of Character," *Vogue,* April 1990.

Bonnie Churchhill, "Just a Normal Girl-Next-Door Superstar," *Christian Science Monitor,* May 28, 1999.

Steve Daly, "The Fighting Irish: Liam Neeson and Director Neil Jordan Waged a 12-year Battle of Their Own to Bring the Story of Controversial Irish Revolutionary Michael Collins to the Screen—and the Rest Is History," *Entertainment Weekly,* October 18, 1996.

Deidre Donahue, "Even with the Coca-Cola Kid, Things Aren't Going Better for Eric Roberts—Just Ask Him," *People Weekly,* September 10, 1985.

Andrew Essex, "Acting Aces Susan Sarandon and Julia Roberts Go Head-to-Head in the Holiday Family Tearjerker *Stepmom*—and They're Still Speaking!" *Entertainment Weekly,* November 27, 1998.

Myra Forsberg, "Julia Roberts Faces a Character Test," *New York Times,* March 19, 1990.

Juliann Garey, "The Real Julia," *Redbook,* April 2001.

Doug Garr, "Family Ties: Scene Three: Though They Are an Acting Family, Eric, Julia and Lisa Roberts Aren't Cut from the Typical Hollywood Mold," *Harper's Bazaar,* February 1989.

Melina Gerosa, "Fascinating Talk with Fascinating Women," *Ladies Home Journal,* January 1999.

Melina Gerosa, "Truly Julia," *Ladies Home Journal,* September 1995.

Jeff Giles, "The 20 Million Dollar Woman," *Newsweek,* March 13, 2000.

Jeff Gordinier, "Living the Life of Reilly," *Entertainment Weekly,* February 23, 1996.

Jeff Gordinier, "The Next Julia Roberts," *Entertainment Weekly,* August 11, 1995.

Mark Harris, "Julia Roberts," *Entertainment Weekly,* June 24, 1994.

Chris Heath, "Portrait of a Trash-Talking Lady," *Rolling Stone,* April 13, 2000.

J.D. Heyman, "Too Good to Be True," *US Weekly,* July 16, 2001.

Brian D. Johnson, "Dolled Up in Dixie," *Maclean's,* November 20, 1989.

James Kaplan, "A Starlet Is Born," *Rolling Stone,* January 12, 1989.

Barry Koltnow, "Actor Says New Movie Shows He's Putting More Emphasis on Quality Roles," Knight-Ridder/Tribune News Service, March 25, 1996.

Dean Lamanna and Susan Price, "Down Home with Julia and Lyle," *Ladies Home Journal,* February 1994.

Shelley Levitt, "Hidden Star," *People Weekly,* February 8, 1991.

Shelley Levitt, "Lovett First Sight," *People Weekly,* July 12, 1993.

Lorrie Lynch, "Julia Roberts Is Back This Weekend in *My Best Friend's Wedding,*" *USA Weekend,* June 20–22, 1997.

Leslie Marshall, "Ain't Life Grand? Or, Rather, Ain't Her Life Grand?" *In Style,* March 1, 2001.

Leslie Marshall, "Don't Fence Her In," *In Style,* January 1, 2000.

Nancy Mills, "Woman of Steel: Julia Roberts," *Cosmopolitan,* November 1989.

Ralph Novak, *Satisfaction,* reviewed in *People Weekly,* Feb. 29, 1988.

Ralph Novak, *Something to Talk About,* reviewed in *People Weekly,* August 21, 1995.

Sally Ogle Davis, "Julia Roberts, Shooting Star," *Ladies Home Journal,* July 1991.

Anne-Marie O'Neill et al, "Their Separate Ways," *People Weekly,* July 16, 2001.

Lawrence O'Toole, *Ready to Wear,* reviewed in *Entertainment Weekly,* June 9, 1995.

People Weekly, "Calling It Off: Julia Roberts and Kiefer Sutherland Put the Wedding on Hold," June 24, 1991.

People Weekly, "Julia Roberts," May 9, 1994.

People Weekly, "Julia Roberts," May 14, 2001.

People Weekly, "Julia Roberts: Playing Hooker or Tink, the Pretty Woman Filmgoers Love to Love Learns About the Dark Side of Fame," December 30, 1991.

Steve Pond, "Pretty Woman Indeed," *Rolling Stone,* August 9, 1990.

Susan Price, "Julia, Her Lessons in Love," *Ladies Home Journal,* June 1994.

Jill Rachlin and Jeff Robin, "*The Steel Magnolias* Scrap Book," *Ladies Home Journal,* November 1989.

David Rensin, "Julia Makes Trouble," *Rolling Stone,* July 14, 1994.

Ira Robbins, "Heaven's Prisoners," *Entertainment Weekly,* November 5, 1996.

Leah Rozen, *Everyone Says I Love You,* reviewed in *People Weekly,* January 20, 1997.

Richard Schickel, *Conspiracy Theory,* reviewed in *Time,* August 18, 1997.

Susan Schindehette, "The Jewel Who's Julia," *People Weekly,* September 17, 1990.

Karen S. Schneider, "One Last Sad Song," *People Weekly,* April 10, 1995.

Karen S. Schneider et al, "Then and Wow!" *People Weekly,* March 20, 2000.

Michael Segell, "Julia Roberts: Still Falling in Love with Love," *Cosmopolitan,* July 1996.

Marshall Sella, "Julia Tells a Lie," *Harper's Bazaar,* March 2000.

Kevin Sessums, "The Crown Julia," *Vanity Fair,* October 1993.

Kyle Smith, "A Star Brightens," *People Weekly,* July 7, 1997.

Liz Smith, "Julia Settles In," *Good Housekeeping,* August 2001.

Liz Smith, "The Joys of Julia," *Good Housekeeping,* August 1999.

Leo Standora, "Julia Roberts Tells Letterman She Still Loves Bratt," Knight-Ridder/Tribune News Service, July 10, 2001.

J. Randy Taraborrelli, "Pretty Strong Woman," *Good Housekeeping,* September 1997.

Alex Tresniowski et al, "Julia Roberts: ACTRESS. (The 50 Most Beautiful People in the World 2000)," *People Weekly,* May 8, 2000.

Mike Turner, "Up for an Oscar, Julia Plays it Cool and Pushes Her Newest Film," Knight-Ridder/Tribune News Service, March 2, 2001.

Mal Vincent, "*The Mexican* Star Julia Roberts Basks in Her Oscar Nomination," Knight-Ridder/Tribune News Service, February 28, 2001.

Stephen Whitty, *My Best Friend's Wedding,* reviewed in *Entertainment Weekly,* December 12, 1997.

Websites

The City of Smyrna (www.ci.smyrna.ga.us). Information on Julia's hometown.

The Gale Group Biography Resource Center (galenet.gale group.com). This resource contains biographies on numerous celebrities, including Julia Roberts, Liam Neeson, and Dylan McDermott.

The Numbers (www.the-numbers.com). Provides box office data for a variety of films.

Films

Satisfaction, Twentieth Century Fox, 1988.

Index

Picture Credits

About the Author

Terri Dougherty is a freelance writer from Appleton, Wisconsin. In addition to nonfiction books for children, she also writes magazine and newspaper articles. A native of Black Creek, Wisconsin, Terri graduated from Seymour High School and the University of Wisconsin-Oshkosh. She was a reporter and editor at the *Oshkosh Northwestern* daily newspaper for five years before beginning her freelance writing career. In her spare time Terri plays soccer and reads. She enjoys cross-country skiing and attending plays with her husband, Denis, and swimming, biking, and playing with their three children, Kyle, Rachel, and Emily.